CALLAN ABRAHAMS

# What I Know Until Now

FAINOM PUBLISHERS

CALLAN ABRAHAMS

# What I Know Until Now

FAINOM
PUBLISHERS

*First published by Fainom Publishers 2025*



*Contact Details:*
*Website: WhatIKnowUntilNow.com*
*Email: cal@whatIknowUntilnow.com*
*Socials: @Callan_Cay*

*First edition*

*ISBN: 9781991269577*

*This book was professionally typeset on Reedsy.*
*Find out more at reedsy.com*

*To Jordan and Jorja,*

*May you always know how deeply you are loved and never doubt your brilliance or your place in this world.*

*You are capable of greatness, but more than that, you are enough—exactly as you are. Live boldly, love fiercely, and chase the things that set your soul on fire.*

*Never shrink, never quiet your dreams, and always believe in the magic within you.*
*With all my love,*

*Aunty Callan* ❤

# Contents

# 1

# Isn't she lovely

## Born Free

On **10 May 1994**, the same day Nelson Mandela took the oath of office as South Africa's first democratically elected president, I was born. A little **coloured baby girl** arrived into a world that was shifting, transforming, and redefining itself. **Freedom had finally come**, but the weight of what came before still lingered in the air, thick and unshakable.

To truly understand what this day meant for my family and for South Africa, you have to go back. I have watched enough documentaries to know that if you want to understand a person, you need to start with their **parents**—maybe even their **grandparents**.

## A Legacy of Strength

Strong women run in my family. Not just on one side but both.

Let's start with my grandmother, **Stella "Star" Green-Thompson**. The name alone should tell you everything. She was the **life of the party**, an **unapologetically vibrant** personality, and a fiercely independent woman before it was even a trend. She had a **larger-than-life presence**, the kind that made her unforgettable.

Her father, a Portuguese immigrant from Madeira, could barely speak English when he arrived in South Africa. Life was not kind to him—he lost his wife while his children were still young, leaving them without a mother's embrace to soften the world. **With no other choice, my grandmother and her brother were sent to a Catholic convent**, a place that would shape much of her childhood. It was not an easy life. But despite the hardships, despite the loss, despite growing up without parents to guide her, she emerged from it all **charming, beautiful, and strong**—a **deadly combination in a woman**.

Of course, Fire needs Ice, so she marries Herbert Green-Thompson. He was a hardworking, honest, and good man with Scottish ancestry, which allowed him to pass as white. I know very little about him, but I know he was a quiet, humble man who loved gardening and gave up everything his wealthy family offered to be with my grandmother.

On my father's side, my grandmother **Sylvia Abrahams** also found her peace in **gardening**. It was right up there with her love for God, baking, and cooking. She had an unwavering faith, one that could not be shaken, no matter what life threw at her. I like to believe that **her prayers are still covering me today**. She was always busy, always moving, always working on something. Looking back, I suspect she had a bit of **ADHD** too. **She could not sit still, and her hands always needed to be doing something.**

But more than that, **she was love personified**. She was the kind of woman who poured into people. She had an enormous impact on her community, and she gave so much of herself to the people around her.

Then, there was **George Abrahams**, my grandfather. He was a **choir conductor** at his Anglican church, **Saint Gabriel's**, a man whose life revolved around music. He played **bass** in a band for many years during his youth. He was also a man who **loved Christmas more than anything else**.

And when I say he loved Christmas, I do not mean in a casual, "I like this holiday" way. **No, my grandfather started planning his Christmas lunch in June**. He saved up for months to ensure that his family had only the best on that day. Christmas was the **one day he could give them everything he knew they deserved.**

## The Man Who Raised Me

That same **unwavering commitment and devotion to family** was passed down to my father. There was **nothing** he would not do for us. Every **cent, every moment, every ounce of his being** was dedicated to his family. He was **the strong, silent type**, a man who never made a fuss but whose presence was always felt.

**To the world, he was Coach Rainier.**

He was not just my inspiration—he was an **inspiration to many soccer boys who needed a role model**. I wish I had understood the significance of what he was doing at the time. Maybe I would have been more patient and more understanding.

My father was **the opposite of every coloured male stereotype you have ever heard**. And the truth is, he was not an anomaly. It sometimes feels like we forget to acknowledge how many men like him exist in our communities.

I grew up watching him approach **every problem with quiet logic**. If something broke in the house, he would not immediately rush to fix it. He would sit, think for fifteen minutes, sketch a plan, and then start working. He was not just fixing things—he was **designing solutions**.

And when it came to raising me, he took the same approach. He wanted me to think for myself.

My father has been a data analyst at Metro Bus for decades. Some might say that data runs in the family. At a very young age he introduced me to computers. In fact, challenging me to take one apart and put it back together again. He allowed me to do his data capturing on excel spreadsheets as a child. I learned to understand the significance of every single data input. Making sure the data was correct and clean was my only mission.

Every morning on the way to school, he played **702 Talk Radio** and would encourage endless debates. He asked my opinion, and whether I was **right or wrong did not matter**—what mattered was that I **had an opinion**. Over time, I learned to **engage with the world** and to have a perspective. Over time, I wanted to know more. I paid attention to politics, legal amendments, economic shifts, and global events. **I was expected to understand the world, not just exist in it.** I was expected **not just to know things but to form my own thoughts about them**.

## My Super Woman

My mother, **Lenise Abrahams**, was a **corporate international banker**.

My mother **dreamed of becoming an air hostess**, but she was told she was **too short** for the role. Instead of letting that stop her, she worked **odd jobs**, saving every cent for **her big move to Johannesburg**—a leap of faith toward a better life. With **grit and determination**, she carved out a place for herself in the corporate world, starting her banking career at **Standard Bank**, where she was among **the first non-white employees** to step into a space that had long been closed to people like her. Most of her career was spent at **ABN Amro Bank**, where she worked until they left South Africa. She did everything: compliance, payments, guarantees. She loved that the bank was small because it allowed her to move between departments, constantly learning and adapting. The variety kept her engaged—staying in one place too long would have been unbearable. She thrived on new challenges and, in hindsight, possibly a reflection of undiagnosed ADHD.

But make no mistake—**she worked hard.**

She left the house at **5 AM** every morning, long before the sun had risen, and didn't return home until **6 or 7 PM**. Day in and day out, she committed herself fully to her work, navigating the relentless demands of corporate banking with precision and determination. She wasn't just good at what she did—she was exceptional. While others focused on survival, she pushed herself to **master** every aspect of her job.

She made it look effortless, but at the end of the day, I saw the exhaustion in her eyes. I saw the sacrifices. I saw how much she gave, not just to her job but to us. **She carried it all without ever letting it show.**

She loved what she did, and I loved **watching her do it**.

My younger brother Jared and I went to work with my mum quite often. Jared and I were complete opposites. He was a brilliant sportsman and I couldn't even run in a straight line. We would ride the **414 bus** for two hours to **Sandton**, sitting through the long trip just to spend the day under her desk. The journey was long, but the reward was always worth it—a fancy **bacon and egg sandwich** and hot chocolate from the canteen. I looked forward to those days although I'm sure that my brother would have preferred to be on the football field. Those days at mum's work place felt well worth it because I got to **watch her in action**.

Growing up, my mother would say that she worked with "clowns". And I can confirm that I was very disappointed to find out that there were indeed; no clowns. I know, I looked.

She walked through the office with **effortless confidence**, greeting everyone and commanding attention without demanding it.

If she was asked to present at the last minute, she would stand up and **speak off the cuff, never breaking a sweat**.

I was mesmerized.

That was my mom. My **idol**.

Her shoes, her bags, her presence—**it was all magic to me**.

## A different time...

My grandparents were born into a world that **dictated their worth** before they could take their first breath. Their place in society was determined **not by their dreams, skills, or ambitions** but by something they had no control over—the colour of their skin.

They came into a South Africa that **did not see them as fully human**. They were people but not citizens. They were workers but not equals. The system did not ask what they could contribute or what they aspired to be; instead, it **boxed them in**, controlled them, and made sure they knew their place.

The **Group Areas Act** dictated where they could live—**not in neighborhoods of opportunity but in crowded, isolated townships**, where roads were left broken and houses built more like containment units than homes. The **Bantu Education Act** ensured their children—my parents—would never receive the same education as white children. Schools were **deliberately underfunded**, classrooms were overcrowded, and teachers were given a curriculum designed **not to uplift but to limit.** And that's only If they had a school built for them at all.

It didn't stop at housing or education. The government controlled every aspect of their existence. Laws dictated **where they could walk, where they could sit, and who they could love**. And if they resisted? The state responded with force. **Police raids were common**, and entire communities were uprooted overnight—families were forced from their homes, and entire neighborhoods were erased like they had never existed.

They lived under surveillance, under control, under the crushing weight of a system that wanted to keep them small. And for the most part, the world moved on as if their suffering was invisible.

Yet, **they endured**. They learned to survive in a reality that refused to see them as equal. Their lives were shaped by scarcity, resilience, and an unspoken understanding that this was simply **the way things were**—whether they accepted it or not.

## The Generation That Refused to Stay Silent

Then came my parents' generation.

They were born into a world where the **fight against apartheid was no longer a quiet endurance but an open resistance**.

They were still **children** when the **Soweto Uprising** exploded onto the streets. Kids just like them—some as young as 12—were shot dead for daring to demand an education that would give them a future. My parents' generation watched as **hope and fear stood side by side**—where the whispers of revolution were met with the crack of police batons and the stinging burn of tear gas.

The government, desperate to control the inevitable, **tried to manipulate them**. In the 1980s, it introduced the **Tricameral Parliament**, a political system designed to create the illusion of inclusion while keeping real power firmly in white hands. My parents' generation saw through it. They knew better.

The **coloured and Indian communities rejected the system outright**, refusing to participate in elections that would only divide and weaken the broader anti-apartheid movement. Many boycotted the elections entirely, and the system **collapsed before it could ever become legitimate**.

By the time the **1990s** arrived, my parents had **lived through states of emergency, township riots, mass arrests, and brutal crackdowns**. The government was crumbling under the weight of its own oppression. And then, in an event that had once seemed impossible—**Mandela was released.**

The South Africa they had always known **began to crack apart at the seams**.

## The Day They Became Free

In **1994**, my parents stood in line to vote **for the first time in their lives**. For decades, they had been told that their voices did not matter, that they would never have a say in the future of their country. But there they stood—**my mother, heavily pregnant with me, waiting to claim a future that had always been denied to them.**

They cast their votes for **freedom**, for **dignity**, for **something better than what they had known.** But while the laws had changed, **the scars of what they had lived through remained**.

The weight of the past could not be erased with a single election. It **lingered**, passed down **in stories, silences, and the way parents held onto their children just a little too tightly**—hoping, praying, that the world we were born into would be **kinder than the one they had survived**.

So before we move on... maybe **read that first paragraph again**.

My parents are from Wentworth, Durban—a coloured community shaped by forced removals and apartheid segregation. It's a tough place where people work hard; however, opportunities are scarce. Crime and poverty are part of daily life, and many families have to fight to get by. Then there's the oil refinery—built first, with Coloured and Indian people placed next to it later. It's hard to believe how the Apartheid Government placed entire communities right next to a massive industrial site and expected them to live with daily pollution while industry thrived at their expense. Wentworth still exists, and so does the fight for better living conditions.

I didn't grow up there, though. My childhood unfolded in Johannesburg Roodepoort, in a previously middle-income whites-only suburb named Lindhaven. Later, the area became filled with a mix of cultures, incomes, and expectations. Compared to my cousins—mostly boys hardened by Wentworth's realities—I was sheltered and even privileged.

## Chest Baby

When I was a baby, my father held me against his chest every night as if the closeness could protect me from the world. His heartbeat became my lullaby, his voice my reassurance. And the music was always playing. *Isn't she lovely? Isn't she wonderful? Isn't she precious?*

Stevie Wonder's voice filled the house as my father swayed, cradled me, and sang along. Growing up, I was curious, relentless, and constantly asked *why.* My mother used to say I was *sixty at six,* speaking like I had already lived many other lives.

My personality was big, and my energy was endless—but only until I went to preschool. That's when I realized I was different. That's when I started AuDHD masking—something I wouldn't have the words for until I was diagnosed at 30.

I had what is called an *autistic stare*—a long, unblinking gaze that made people uncomfortable. I hadn't known it was unusual until other kids started noticing and pointing it out. That moment changed everything. I learned quickly that being different makes you a target. And so I tried to figure out what *normal* was. I studied people, mirrored them, and forced myself to shrink, to blend in. I became shy—not because I was, but because I didn't know how to exist any other way.

I spent my entire school career trying to fit in, failing, and getting bullied for it. And when the world outside felt unbearable, my own mind wasn't much kinder. Some nights, it wouldn't let me rest. The world was too bright, too noisy, and too much. My skin prickled when I felt my clothes. The hum of the fridge in the kitchen felt like thunder, and the flickering of a light bulb felt like lightning in my brain. I would lie awake, wide-eyed, for days. My body begged for sleep, but my mind was a riot of sensations, refusing to shut down. For years, I became the quiet one. The shy one. But I wasn't shy. I was studying the world, trying to figure out what was considered 'normal' so I could survive in it. And that constant effort to be something I wasn't? It was exhausting.

To this day, I have a habit of **slipping into my mother's shoes**—literally. We wear the same size, and whenever I see her flip-flops lying around, I instinctively put them on. It's a small, familiar comfort, but deep down, I know exactly where it comes from.

As a child, I **didn't want to be me**. I didn't want to be different. I didn't want to be the one who had a mind that struggled to be still, who felt overwhelmed by sounds, who overthought every social interaction. I didn't have the words for it back then, but I do now—**the full extent of my "problems" was AuDHD**. I wasn't less than. I was simply wired differently. But back then, all I knew was that **I wanted to be like them**.

I can still hear my **six-year-old self whispering the wishes she carried like prayers**.

*"I want to be as smart as my dad."*
*"I want to be as confident as my mom."*

I thought if I just **copied them perfectly, if I learned to fit into the mold of who they were**, I would eventually feel like I belonged in the world.

But what I couldn't see then—what I know now—is that **I was never meant to fit into their shoes.** I was meant to walk my own path.

I am **my ancestors' wildest dreams**. Everything that once made me feel different, everything that made me feel like I didn't belong—**it is exactly what they fought for**.

This is what **apartheid struggle heroes dreamed of** when they marched, when they resisted, when they dared to demand more. **They fought so that one day, a person like me would be seen as fully human.** So that I could have access to healthcare that was once denied to us. So that I could **dream beyond survival and exist freely in a world that once tried to erase us**.

And now, in 2025 South Africa, a late-diagnosed coloured woman with AuDHD has the right to **access support and resources**—something that once would have been unimaginable.

**What a victory that is in itself.**

## The Truth I Never Knew

Getting diagnosed with **AuDHD (Autism + ADHD)** as an adult was like finding the missing pages of a book I'd been reading my whole life. Suddenly, everything made sense: the struggles, the anxiety, the exhaustion, the way I had spent my entire existence **overcompensating for what I thought was brokenness**.

But here's what I know until now: I was never broken. I was simply different. And different is not a flaw.

## What This Means for You

If you've ever felt like you don't quite fit, if you've ever questioned why you seem to experience the world differently than others, if you've ever **tried to mold yourself into something you're not** just to be accepted—let me tell you something I wish someone had told me:

***You are not broken.***

The world may not always understand you, but that doesn't mean you don't belong in it.

And as for me?

I'm done hiding.

This book is my unmasking.

It's a love letter to **every misfit, every outlier, every person who has ever felt like they had to shrink themselves into a neat box to survive or fit in.**

What I know until now is this:

**You are not broken. You never were.**

# 2

# What A Difference A Day Makes

I was never someone who just accepted answers—I needed to know *why*. It wasn't just curiosity. It was a force. A hunger. A restless, **urgent need** to understand everything.

It wasn't enough to be told that something worked a certain way—I needed to **break it apart, study the insides, and put it back together again** in my mind. I needed to know *why* that rule applied but another didn't. *Why* did that method work here but not there? *Why* the world functioned the way it did.

And I didn't have the patience to wait for someone else to explain it. School moved **too slow**. It followed a **schedule, a curriculum, and a controlled flow of knowledge** that never matched the pace my brain demanded.

So, I went ahead without it.

## Restless Nights, Racing Thoughts

Sleep? That was something other people did.

At night, when the house was finally quiet, and the world outside had settled into stillness, my mind refused to do the same. While everyone else drifted into rest, my brain was wide awake, running at full speed, refusing to slow down.

One thought would spiral into ten more, one question into a dozen. I would replay entire lessons in my head, dissecting them, searching for patterns, and making sense of things that refused to make sense during the day. If I had a book, I devoured it. If I didn't, I found something—anything—to occupy my mind, because the alternative was lying there, trapped in my own thoughts, watching the hours pass while my body begged for sleep that never came.

Mornings weren't about waking up refreshed; they were just a reset. A brief moment where my body tricked itself into thinking it could function again, even though I was running on two, maybe five hours of broken sleep. I got used to it. I didn't complain. This was just **my normal.**

I never told my parents. They had no idea that every morning when they saw me awake and ready for school, I had already lived an entire night inside my own head.

I was just trying to keep up with my own mind.

## Hiding My Brokenness

My parents never knew. They never saw the mental exhaustion, the racing thoughts, the way my body screamed for rest while my mind refused to shut down.

I never showed them how hard I worked to keep up, how much energy it took just to **exist** in a world that never felt made for me, how much I struggled to hold it together, or how much effort it took to mask my differences—to act normal, to blend in, to be the child they thought I was.

**I made sure of it**.

Because, in my mind, **this was normal**. This was just life. And I assumed **everyone else was doing the same**.

## Mornings Were War Zones

Every morning started with a battle. I was always running late. No matter how early I woke up, no matter how hard I tried to be on time, **something always went wrong**.

I'd misplace my school books. I'd lose my hairbrush. I'd put on one shoe, get distracted, and forget where I left the other. I'd forget my lunchbox in the fridge, my blazer in my room, my schoolwork on my desk. Then I'd rush around in a panic, frantically searching through every drawer, every bag, trying to pull everything together before my parents had a chance to notice the chaos I had created for myself.

My mother, already exhausted from her long hours at work, would sigh in frustration. "Callan! You need to be more organized." I nodded. I agreed. I promised to do better.

But **how could I fix something when I didn't even understand why it was happening?** I just knew that **no matter what I did, I was always behind.**

## The Weight of Perfection

I didn't want my parents to **worry** or think I was **broken**. I saw how **hard they worked** and how much they sacrificed to give me a good life.

They didn't need **another problem to fix**.

So, I became the "easy child."

The **overachiever**. The **rule-follower**. The child who **never needed help**. I did my homework early. I kept my school books neat. I never forgot to hand in assignments. I never got in trouble at school. Because the alternative was **letting them see how much I was struggling**. And that wasn't an option.

## They Never Knew

For **thirty years**, they had no idea. No idea that I spent my nights **awake, staring at the ceiling**. No idea how hard I worked to **keep up with a world that never slowed down for me**.

No idea how much energy it took to appear normal, to pretend I was fine, to hide how much I was drowning. They didn't know because I didn't know either. I thought everyone felt like this. I thought everyone was fighting this invisible battle. I thought I was just bad at life.

## An Old Soul in a Child's Body

I wasn't like other kids. I didn't play outside much. I didn't join in the typical schoolyard games. Instead, I was **obsessed** with making things—**painting, drawing, beading, candle-making, mosaics, and upcycling random junk into art**. My brain **craved stimulation**.

The hyperfocus from Autism meant that when I was interested in something, I would **go all in until I mastered it**. You might think raising me was **easy**. My parents certainly like to say it was. *"Callan was so easy. She did her homework early. She even collected clock busters from teachers."* I think they've forgotten how many items they had to replace because I lost them and how many times they had to tell me to clean my **junkyard of a room**—a room that never stayed clean for more than a day.

It wasn't that I didn't try. I would start with the best intentions, determined to organize everything neatly. But within hours, the chaos would return. **That's ADHD.** I'd pull something out to use, get distracted, and forget to put it back. I'd start tidying one section, then suddenly remember something else I needed to do, leaving the task half-finished. My room was an explosion of unfinished projects, scattered books, half-done crafts, and papers covered in ideas that I never got around to completing.

To me, it made sense. I knew where everything was—until I didn't. I was constantly losing things, turning the place upside down looking for them, only to find them in the most *obvious* places hours later. And the cycle repeated, over and over again.

I was the teacher's pet. Why not? The teachers were the only ones having real conversations The truth was, I had no friends. When I did, It didn't last long before I was kicked out of the group. Breaks? I spent most of them reading alone. Day in, day out. I wished, hoped, that one day I'd have a real friend—someone who didn't think I was weird. Someone who wanted to talk about global politics and the interest rate instead of whatever normal kids talked about.

## We Become What We Absorb

There's a well-known saying in the data world:

> ***"Garbage data in, garbage business insights out."***

I think human beings work the same way.

We are a product of what we consume. The music we listen to, the books we read, the conversations we engage in, the environments we grow up in—it all shapes us, often in ways we don't even realize.

**I was lucky**.

I attended **Model C schools** for both primary and high school. These were schools that were previously "whites-only" middle income schools. It wasn't always easy, and I was often the odd one out, but it gave me access to **good teachers, well-equipped classrooms, and opportunities my parents never had.**

Primary school was where I was first introduced to structured learning, different cultures, and high academic expectations. There were sports, school trips, and science competitions—experiences that made learning exciting, not just something you did because you had to. But if there was one school event that truly ignited something in me, it was Grade 7 Market Day.

## Foamies, Beading, and the Entrepreneurial Bug

Market Day was supposed to be a **once-off school event**—a fun little exercise to teach kids the basics of business. For me?

It was the launch of **my first empire.**

I **obliterated the competition.**

My product? **Foamies.** They were **colourful foam cards** decorated with names, cute illustrations, and personalized designs. I made them with cats, dogs, butterflies, and cars—you name it. My classmates **loved them.** Sales were so good that I **kept selling them for months** after Market Day ended.

And when demand eventually slowed down? I **pivoted.**

I moved on to **exotic, advanced beading**. But I wasn't just stringing plastic beads together—I was working with **Swarovski crystals, needle, and cotton,** creating intricate, high-end designs.

Why? Because the more **elaborate** the design, the **higher** the price.

The more **value** I put into my product, the more I could **charge.**

Simple **economics.**

There was just one problem—**my school teachers couldn't afford my talent.** So, I **expanded my market.** I took my products to **my mother's co-workers**, where my audience had **disposable income** and **poor gift-planning skills**.

My highest sale? **R1,200.** A husband who had forgotten his anniversary, and my "salesperson" (aka **my mom**) knew **exactly** how to use desperation to close a deal.

I was **13 years old.**

Was this child labour? **Not at all. This was entrepreneurship.** This was **passion. I loved the thrill of the deal.** What can I say? I was a strange child.

I lived for **arts and crafts, design, and creating something out of nothing.** Today my favourite craft is working with artificial intelligence.

It's the same process when you think about it; Art and science working together to create something new. Something people need.

I follow this process: Ideate. Design. Express. Create. Execute. Master. Deliver the end result.

Deep down, I think I always knew—I wasn't just having fun. I was learning how to build something for myself.

## Old Afrikaans Ladies & Sharing a Passion

Looking back, I did make some *real hardcore* friends as a child—just not in the way you'd expect. While other kids my age were hanging out with their classmates, I found my people in the most unexpected place. Do you know who also adored arts and crafts? A room full of **old Afrikaans white ladies with whom I regularly took beadwork classes**.

Every week, I sat with them, carefully threading tiny crystals onto delicate wire, drinking tea, eating quiche, and soaking in their stories. They spoke about their children, their lives, and the things they had learned over the years. In those moments, I wasn't the odd one out. I wasn't the weird child who struggled to fit in at school. To them, I was just a sweet little girl who asked far too many questions, always curious, always eager to learn. And when I wasn't there, they noticed. They missed me.

## Sensory Overload & The Desperation to Keep Up

Grade 10. The shuffling of chairs, the tapping of pens, the endless talking and laughing—it never stopped. The classroom was never silent, never still. Even when the teacher spoke, there was always something happening in the background. The flick of a page, the zip of a pencil case, the clinking of a ruler against a desk.

The lights buzzed too loudly, the air felt stiff, the desks were hard and uncomfortable. The sound of chalk scraping against the board made my teeth clench. I wanted to focus. I wanted to learn. But the noise drowned everything out.

I gripped my pen and forced myself to keep up, but the teacher's words were lost in the chaos. I watched numbers appear on the board, but they didn't connect to anything. It was like watching a puzzle being put together without knowing what the final picture was supposed to look like.

One lesson missed turned into two. Then three. Before I knew it, I was falling behind in Math.

## Math Class Was a Nightmare

I had bad luck with Math classes. Every year, I ended up in a class where the teacher struggled to keep discipline. I don't blame them. Some of them tried their best, but how do you teach algebra when kids are throwing rulers across the room? How do you explain trigonometry when half the class is talking over you?

I sat there, gripping my pen so tightly my fingers hurt, trying to tune out the noise, trying to focus on the lesson, but nothing made sense. Numbers blurred together. Concepts flew past me. And because I didn't want to seem dumb, I never raised my hand to ask for help.

I just sat there, stressed, overwhelmed and lost.

By the time I got home, I was too mentally drained to process what had happened in class. My mind was exhausted from trying to filter out the distractions and pretending to understand. The next day, I would go back, sit at my desk, and do it all over again—still behind, still pretending, still desperate to keep up.

## Finding Solutions – YouTube, Sci-Bono, and Master Maths

By Grade 11, I had reached a breaking point. I couldn't sit in class pretending to understand anymore. I couldn't keep falling behind, hoping things would eventually make sense. I definitely couldn't let Math be the reason my dreams slipped away. A few good Math teachers tried to host extra Math classes, but the same problem remained.

So, I did what I had always done—I found another way. If school wasn't going to provide me with the additional support I needed, I would need to learn how to teach myself.

## YouTube University – Teaching Myself From Scratch

Somewhere along the way, I discovered that YouTube had Math tutorials. And suddenly, everything changed. For the first time, I could pause, rewind, re-watch, and actually absorb the information at my own pace. I could find different explanations for the same problem until something finally clicked. If one teacher didn't make sense, I could find another. I wasn't just using YouTube to study. I was rebuilding my entire education.

Sidebar: To this day, YouTube and I? We go way back! That's where I taught myself Art, History, Chemistry, Economics, Astronomy, Psychology, and whatever else had caught my interest over the years.

Anyway, during this time in my life, however, I was using it to fight for my future. Even with YouTube, I still wasn't where I needed to be.

## Sci-Bono Saturday School – Extra Math for a Child Who Refused to Fail

I needed structure, something closer to an actual classroom, but one where I could actually learn instead of just trying to survive the noise. My teachers put my name forward to join the prestigious Sasol Sci-Bono Saturday School, and after a few compulsory tests, I made it in. Sci-Bono was a science and technology centre in Johannesburg that offered extra Math and Science classes on Saturdays.

So, while most kids were sleeping in, going to the mall, or playing sports, I was waking up early to get to Sci-Bono. For the first time, I sat in a classroom where the teacher could actually teach without disruptions. The students actually wanted to learn, and the lessons actually made sense. I made friends! But they were just as busy as I was trying to get their grades up, preparing to send off University applications. I desperately wanted to go to Wits University. I applied nowhere else. It was Wits or nothing. (Hey, kids! This is a terrible idea. Don't do what I did.)

Sci-bono wasn't a miracle fix, either. I wasn't suddenly acing Math overnight. But at least, for the first time, I was moving forward instead of slipping further behind. Even with Sci-Bono and YouTube, I still wasn't where I needed to be. I needed something more intensive—and fast.

## Master Math - The Sacrifice That Changed Everything

That's when my mother found Master Math, a private tutoring centre offering one-on-one help. It was a chance to finally make sense of the numbers that had haunted me for years.

There was only one problem.

My mother had just been retrenched. Money was tight. She and my father sat down, did the math (ironically), and figured out that they could afford to send me for three months—nothing more.

That was all they could give me. Three months to turn things around. This was my shot. And I wasn't going to waste it.

## The Unexpected Leadership Moment

On my first day at Master Math, I sat down, opened my book, and got straight to work.

I wasn't there to play. I wasn't there to chat. I was there to learn.

But when I looked around, I realized that many of the other students were sitting at the computers, clicking through exercises without asking questions. They had access to tutors, but they weren't using them. I didn't understand it. I had three months to turn things around.

So, I asked every question I had, challenged every method until I understood why it worked and used every second in that room. At first, the other kids ignored me. But over time, something changed. My determination started rubbing off on them.

They started asking their own questions, using the tutors instead of just sitting there and actually caring about improving. And that's when I realized something. You don't need to be old to be a leader. You don't need to be important to have influence. Even if you feel insignificant, what you do still matters. People are watching you—even when you don't realize it. And sometimes, your effort gives others permission to try harder, too.

## A Lesson in Generosity – The Kindness That Changed My Life

When my three months were up, my parents had to pull me out of Master Math. They couldn't afford more lessons.

I had done my best. I had pushed as hard as I could. But I still needed help. A week later, we got a call. It was Neil—the head tutor at Master Math. He asked my mother why I hadn't been coming. She explained our situation. And Neil did something I'll never forget. He told my mother, "Let Callan keep coming. She doesn't have to pay, and we'll cover it."

I wasn't used to people going out of their way to help me. At that moment, I realized something. When you work hard, when you show up, when you put in effort—people notice.

And sometimes, the world gives back in ways you never expected. Master Math didn't just teach me how to pass Matric. It taught me that showing up, pushing yourself, and refusing to quit matters.

One day at a time, one lesson at a time, one act of effort at a time. That's how you change your future.

Looking back, I realize now that my journey wasn't about one big breakthrough. There was no single moment that changed everything. It was built day by day, choice by choice, lesson by lesson. Some days, the progress was small. Some days, it felt like nothing was changing. But every effort eventually stacked up. Every question, every hour spent studying, every decision to keep going—it all added up to something bigger than I could see at the time.

And that's the lesson I take with me now. The restless mind, the one that wouldn't let me sleep, the one that questioned everything, the one that always pushed forward—it's not a burden. It's a fire. And when you learn to direct it, when you channel that urgency into the right things, you don't just survive. You grow. You build.

**You win.**

# 3

# Gramercy Park

We all wear masks.

Some are small, just enough to soften the edges of who we are to make life easier. Others are so well-crafted, so deeply ingrained, that even we forget what's underneath. But masking is exhausting. It is a performance we do every day, for people who often wouldn't even notice if we stopped. And yet, we keep going, afraid of what might happen if the world saw us for who we really are.

## The Curse of Being "Outgrown"

I've been outgrown more times than I can count.

It's not like losing friends in the usual way, where a fallout happens or an argument sets you apart. No, being outgrown is quieter, slower. It creeps up on you. One day, you're laughing with someone, sharing inside jokes, feeling like you belong. The next, you're too much. Too deep. Too different. Too childish.

And suddenly, you realize they've left you behind.

I've spent my whole life watching friendships slip away, not because I did anything wrong, but because I couldn't keep up with the unspoken social script of growing up. One moment, we were all playing in the sand, imagining kingdoms and stories. The next, the rules changed. The things we were supposed to care about changed. What we were supposed to like, talk about, and prioritize changed.

But no one gave me the memo. I never lost friends. They just eventually outgrew me. They moved on while I was still trying to figure out what I was supposed to be interested in now.

Learning to mask isn't a one-time thing. It's a lifelong adjustment. Just when you think you've figured out how to fit in, everyone moves on to the next stage of life, and you're left behind—scrambling to catch up, relearning the script, rewriting yourself to be acceptable again.

It wasn't until years later that I realized what was really happening. I wasn't childish. I wasn't emotionally stunted. I was autistic. And masking was the only thing keeping me from being completely alone.

But I wasn't the first to wear a mask.

## The Obsession with Egypt

National Geographic used to have "Egypt Week" right after "Shark Week," and I was hooked. I would sit in front of the TV, completely hypnotized by the world of the pharaohs. I wasn't just interested—I was obsessed.

Ancient Egypt was a civilization of impossible brilliance, filled with grand structures, powerful rulers, and knowledge that seemed to stretch beyond time. Every artifact, every hieroglyph, every story felt like a piece of something bigger, something I desperately wanted to understand.

And in the middle of it all, one name stood out.

**Hatshepsut.**

She wasn't just another ruler. She wasn't just another pharaoh. She was the **King.**

## Hatshepsut: The Woman Who Became King

Hatshepsut's story was different from every other Egyptian ruler I had read about. She wasn't just another Queen. She wasn't a mere placeholder until a man came to take over. She ruled in her own right, not as a wife or a mother, but as Pharaoh—God's chosen ruler of Kemet.

But Egypt wasn't ready for a woman to sit on the throne. So, she did what she had to do. She became something they could accept. She wore the royal beard, dressed in traditional pharaonic clothing, and had herself depicted as a man in statues and inscriptions. She blurred the line between King and Queen, ruler and woman. She played the game with such precision that history almost erased her.

But make no mistake—she was not pretending. Hatshepsut built temples that still stand today. She led military campaigns. She expanded trade and wealth beyond what Egypt had seen in generations. She didn't just sit on the throne—she **ruled**. She played the role they needed her to play, but she did it on her own terms.

**She was the King**.

And I understood her in a way I couldn't explain at the time.

## The Mask of a Female Pharaoh & The Mask of a Neurodivergent Child

Hatshepsut had to perform a version of herself that the world would accept. She had to walk a tightrope between being true to herself and being the ruler Egypt needed her to be. I knew exactly what that felt like. Because I did the same thing every single day.

I had spent years being the version of myself that made other people comfortable. The agreeable one. The one who didn't didn't push too hard and didn't take up too much space. The one who measured every word before speaking. The one who smiled when she was supposed to, even when she wanted to scream.

The weight of a mask is heavy, and over time, it suffocates. It dulls you, until one day you wake up and realize that you have lost yourself entirely. The real you—the one with unfiltered thoughts, unpolished edges, and unshaken truths—has been buried beneath layers of social conditioning and expectation.

Hatshepsut masked so she could rule. I masked so I could survive. But what happens when you spend too long pretending?

## The Cost of Masking

Masking doesn't just hurt the person wearing it. It hurts everyone. When we pretend to be something we're not, we feed into a world that values performance over authenticity. A world where people are too afraid to be honest. A world where we praise perfection instead of truth, conformity instead of individuality. And that is how we end up here—trapped in systems that are built on illusion.

Look around. So much of what is broken in this world comes from people pretending. Leaders who pretend they care while making decisions that harm the most vulnerable. Companies that pretend to value people but extract everything they can from them. A society that preaches kindness but rewards cruelty. And beneath it all, individuals pretending to be okay when they are not.

## Sia: The Wisdom of Seeing Through the Illusion

In ancient Kemet, the concept of **Sia** was about divine perception—the ability to see beyond illusions and understand the truth of oneself and the world.

But masking is the opposite of Sia. It is the act of blinding ourselves, of making sure no one sees the truth beneath the surface. The longer we wear the mask, the harder it becomes to recognize what is real.

What happens when an entire society loses Sia? When no one truly sees, only performs? We end up where we are now—disconnected, directionless, drowning in expectations that serve no one.

But we don't have to stay here. We don't have to keep up the act.

## A Moment of Truth

Something inside of me always knew that masking was wrong. Lying—pretending to be someone I wasn't—felt fundamentally off. It gnawed at me, even when I didn't have the words to explain why.

It came to a head when I was a teenager, preparing for my confirmation in the Anglican Church. Part of the process included confession, a moment of deep reflection and truth.

I found myself with Father Gerard Sharp, a man who embodied the pillar-of-the-community type—big build, powerful voice, strong presence, the kind of coloured uncle who commanded respect without even trying. He had that old-school authority, but with the weight of genuine care. Every Sunday, we saw him beat his chest three times before Holy Eucharist as if grounding himself in something deeper than ritual. That day, I understood why.

I confessed. I confessed, through choked-back tears, that I had been lying to everyone, performing a version of myself that felt more like a character than a person. I broke down, completely undone, but I couldn't explain why. I didn't have the language yet for AuDHD masking—I just knew something about my existence felt like a long, exhausting performance. And I hated it.

After confession, while meditating in the stillness of the church garden, all I got from God was this: **One day, you will understand. One day, your story will help others.**

I remember blinking through my tears, completely bewildered. Was I hearing this wrong? Was I failing at religion? (I was pretty sure confession wasn't supposed to feel like receiving a prophecy.)

But even in my confusion, something in me quieted. A knowing.

A trust that, in time, everything would make sense, even if I didn't understand it yet.

## Taking Off the Mask

I completed matric with 5 distinctions and got into Wits to study a BSc in Economic Science and Mathematics —5 distinctions, an exact number I weirdly remember writing about in a Grade 8 essay. Foreshadowing? Or sheer grit?

Unmasking is terrifying. The first time I took off the mask, I began my journey at Wits University. It meant facing parts of myself that I had spent years hiding, and it meant accepting that not everyone will like what they see.

But the alternative is worse: living your whole life behind a mask, never knowing what it feels like to exist freely, fully, and unapologetically.

We all wear masks.

But maybe, just maybe, **it's time to take them off.**

# 4

# Human

## Wits: The Power of the People

I never planned to come out of my shell at Wits.
It just... happened.
Maybe it was inevitable.

Once again, living my ancestor's wildest dreams, there I was—bright red hair, sometimes curly, sometimes straight, worn-out blue jeans, and black boots all year round. Short boots were worn in summer, and long boots were worn in winter. And my black leather jacket, which I wore like armor. Who did I think I was? (Honestly, I still don't know).

There was something about the place—the energy, the diversity, the sheer **intensity of thought**—that pulled you in. You didn't just go to Wits to study. You went to **wake up.** Everywhere you turned, there were people with **big ideas, big ambitions, and**

**big opinions**. Conversations could start with a casual **"Hey, did you do the assignment?"** and, within minutes, spiral into deep debates about economics, philosophy, or the future of South Africa. The university wasn't just a place for learning—it was a place where **ideas clashed, merged, evolved.**

We didn't always agree. In fact, **we rarely agreed.** And that's what made it powerful. Because **when a society learns how to move together—without needing to think the same—we will unlock something unstoppable.**

And at Wits, we were just beginning to discover what that meant.

## Fees Must Fall: The Awakening

At one moment, Wits University was **just a *normal* university**—lectures, assignments, and rushed coffee between classes. Then, it was something **bigger**. The **Fees Must Fall movement** wasn't just a student protest; it was a **shift in consciousness.**

Suddenly, **everything was political.** Who could afford to be there? Who couldn't? Who got left behind? Who had never been given a chance in the first place? And most importantly:

**What were we going to do about it?**
People **chose sides.**
Some friendships never recovered.

Debates spilled out of lecture halls and into the streets. For the first time, many of us realized that power—real power—wasn't something we had to wait for. It was something we could create.

And that was the lesson Wits gave me. **When people move together, they can change the course of history.**

## The Missing Middle & the Hustle for Survival

I was part of the **missing middle**—not poor enough for full financial aid, not rich enough to afford university without struggle. Wits didn't care if I had bus fare to get to class. It didn't care if I couldn't afford textbooks. It didn't care if I was calculating, down to the cent, how to stretch my money to make it through the semester.

And so, like many others, my parents and I **found a way.**

I turned my **math tutoring side hustle** into a full-scale operation. But I wasn't just tutoring—I was **outsourcing tutoring**, connecting struggling students with my smartest friends, taking a cut, and running what was essentially **a decentralized education system within Wits itself.**

I wasn't the only one doing this. Wits was full of students who had taken survival into their own hands, who had figured out how to **build networks, leverage skills, and create value in places where there was none.** We had all learned how to be successful on our own. **What we were only just discovering—what we had never been taught—was the power of community.**

## More Than Just a Meal

The **Matrix** was always alive.

It wasn't just a student mini-mall—it was **the heart of Wits.**

It smelled like **hot chips and fried polony,** the air thick with the scent of cheap, greasy comfort food that kept students fueled between lectures. The sound of fast, overlapping conversations filled the space—political debates at one table, last-minute cramming at another, bursts of laughter from a group sharing a joke between bites.

On some days, **live poetry, spontaneous debates, or street musicians** playing outside would turn an ordinary lunch break into something electric. Big corporate would set up stalls, handing out freebies, trying to capture the attention of students who were too broke to refuse a free energy drink or a pen.

For most, it was **chaotic but exciting.** For me? **It was an assault on the senses.**

The sheer volume of it all—the voices, the movement, the clatter of chairs scraping against the tiles, the weight of too many people in one space—built up **until it felt like my brain was being squeezed.**

So, like clockwork, I'd fake a lecture. I'd grab my bag, nod as if

I had somewhere important to be, and slip away to one of the quieter corners of campus. It wasn't that I didn't want to be part of the moment—it was that my brain simply **couldn't keep up with the intensity of it all.**

But one thing was undeniable. **Food brought people together.**

## Kara Nichas: The Real MVP of the Missing Middle

If you were a broke Wits student, you knew about **Kara Nichas.** It was **the great equalizer.**

It didn't matter whether you were in law, engineering, medicine, or fine arts—when money was tight (and it always was), you found your way there. A chip sandwich? R6. A quarter loaf of bread stuffed with chips and polony? R12.

Kara Nichas kept us going. It wasn't fancy, but it was **consistent, reliable, affordable.** Beyond Kara Nichas, beyond the hot chips and cheap sandwiches, I was about to be introduced to something even more important.

## The Wits Food Programme: A Lesson in Dignity

There's a difference between survival and **being treated like a human being.**

Wits understood this.

The **Wits Food Programme** wasn't just about feeding students who needed help—it was about **protecting dignity.** If you were struggling, you didn't have to stand in a separate line. You didn't have to carry a special token that marked you as someone who couldn't afford a meal. You were encouraged to grab a healthy meal and make real connections in the process. Whether you could afford the Kara Nichas chip sandwich or not.

You just sat down. Students who needed food ate alongside volunteers, so no one could tell who was there to serve and who was there to eat. No pity. No hierarchy. **Just community.** And that's what made it powerful.

It wasn't charity. It wasn't a handout. It was a reminder that community is a basic human right and that social development is everyone's responsibility. Ironically, the network I gained here would drive my personal success later in life more than the coursework itself.

## Community Was Never Meant to Be Charity

Somewhere along the way, our society repackaged 'community' as 'charity'. For thousands of years, societies functioned by helping each other, looking out for those around us, and ensuring that no one was left behind. But capitalism renamed community-building 'charity'—something to look down on, something that made people feel weak for needing help. And the worst part? People believed it.

If you needed assistance, you were made to feel ashamed. If you relied on support, you were told to "pull yourself up by your bootstraps." If you participated in community initiatives, people called it "charity work" instead of "building a better society."

That's never how civilizations thrived.

**Ancient African kingdoms, Indigenous communities, the great empires of the past—they all understood that success was never about the individual. - The law of oneness.**

In ancient Mali, under **Mansa Musa,** wealth wasn't hoarded—it was shared across vast trade networks, ensuring prosperity wasn't just for the elite but for the entire kingdom.

In pre-colonial African societies, the philosophy of **Ubuntu** ("I am because we are") shaped entire ways of life. Communities raised children together, food was shared, and no one was left to struggle alone.

Even the mighty **Roman Empire,** at its peak, had **free grain distribution for the poor**—not out of pity, but because they knew that a starving population would **destabilize the entire empire.**

Yet somewhere in history, we were taught that needing help was a personal failure and giving help was a personal achievement when, in fact, it is the bare minimum you should do as a functioning member of society. Before Wits, I was taught that survival should be the result of individual effort and that we had to prove our worthiness before being given access to basic human needs. Real strength? **It was never about how much you could do alone.**

*It was about how much we could build together.*

At Wits, I saw it firsthand. No one made it alone. Not the students who rationed their last R20 for the week. Not the volunteers at the Wits Food Programme, who served food alongside those they were feeding, nor the wealthier students eating at Olive and Plates every day.

Not even the ones who *seemed* to have it all together—because, in reality, **everyone was carrying something.** When you recognize that, when you embrace it, when you start to **move together instead of apart,** you realize something even bigger.

**The power of the people.**

And when a society moves together?

*There is nothing we can't build.*

## Groove, Balance, and the Art of Knowing Your Limits

If there's one other thing I learned at Wits, it's that **balance is everything.**

There's a myth that the students who lock themselves in their rooms, never go out, and spend every waking hour studying are the ones who succeed. But the university has a way of **humbling even the most disciplined bookworms.** I saw people who never touched alcohol, never went to parties, and never missed a single lecture completely crash and burn under the pressure of it all. And then, there was my friend. (He knows who he is.) This man could Groove (South African Party) from Friday to Sunday evening—sometimes even Monday morning— and somehow still make it to church. During the week? He 'chowed course' (Studied really hard). While others who never left their rooms were failing miserably, he was cruising through his Engineering degree, an **A-student with a perfectly calculated balance between chaos and discipline.**

I respected it.

But me? I ordered my groove, like my steak, '**medium' heat.** I had seen my parents dance at family gatherings, moving to old-school jams, laughing with their friends, and living life with **joy and rhythm.** I had never been taught that success required **suffering** or that fun was the enemy of hard work. I knew that **life was about balance.**

Braam?

Braam had **a pulse, a rhythm, a heartbeat.**

There's something unexplainable about **Groove in the city of Johannesburg.** You'd be in a packed venue, surrounded by complete strangers, yet somehow, everyone was moving together, singing in perfect unison, and feeling the music in the same way.

Groove in South Africa is a spiritual experience. At that age, the spiritual experience seems worth the risk of potentially getting your cell phone stolen by the ''Tik Koppe'' (drug addicts) who were also on the streets.

In these shared moments, nothing else matters—**not your struggles, deadlines, or the stress of university—just the beat, the bass, and the collective energy of people existing fully in the present.** In those moments, there were no rich kids or broke kids, no missing middle, no social hierarchy—**just people connected by something deeper than words.** When people come together—whether to fight, learn, or celebrate—there is power in unity.

But as much as I loved those moments, I knew when to sit at home in my **lab coat (aka my pink gown)** and get to work. Ordering your groove **medium** means knowing your limits. It means knowing when to step into the music and when to step back into the books. It means understanding that **success isn't about choosing between joy and discipline it's about knowing how to hold both.**

## Germany: Seeing Wealth Through a Different Lens

Visiting Germany in my 2nd year was never part of my plan.

At that point, I was still figuring out how to balance academics with my side hustles and stretching every resource I had just to stay in university. The idea of suddenly finding myself halfway across the world, walking through the streets of Tübingen, stepping into the Mercedes-Benz Museum, and learning from some of the most structured, efficient systems in the world? It was surreal.

The opportunity came through SLDU, and I threw myself into the application. I worked *hard* for that trip, filming elaborate videos, crafting an insane application concept, and memorizing German trivia like my life depended on it. This wasn't just about filling out a form—it was about proving to myself that no matter how impossible something seemed, **there was always a way in.**

And when I finally got there?

Germany was everything I had expected—**and nothing like I had expected.**

## Efficiency, Precision, and a Different Kind of Wealth

Everything in Germany felt **ordered.** The streets were clean. The public transport ran on time. The systems worked—**and not just on paper.** It was a level of structure I had never experienced before.

Coming from Johannesburg—where nothing ever ran on time, where there's always an '*-ish*' at the end of every time estimate, where unpredictability is just part of life—it was a complete shift.

I was fascinated. This was what **wealth looked like**—not just in money but in the **ability to trust that the world around you would function the way it was supposed to.** There was no stress about whether the bus would show up, no frustration over failing infrastructure, and no mental gymnastics required just to get through the day.

For a moment, I thought: **This is what equality must feel like.**

## But Even in Wealth, Inequality Exists

Then, one day, I was on a public bus, and a homeless man looked at me, muttered something in German, and then **spat at me. Thankfully, he had bad aim.**

He thought I was Middle Eastern.

At the time, the fear of terrorist attacks was rife around the world, and Europe was experiencing waves of migration from the Middle East, which brought fear, anger, and resentment. To him, I wasn't a student or a visitor; **I was a symbol of something bigger.**

And in that moment, I realized something.

For all the efficiency, all the structure, all the order—**Germany still had people sleeping on the streets.** And to that man? It didn't matter that Germany's inequality was lower than South Africa's. It didn't matter that the statistics showed fewer people in poverty. **Because he was still poor. He was still homeless.**

**He was still angry.**

Sometimes, we look at numbers and think they mean zero.
But there he was.

**Homeless in a country where inequality was agreeably "under control."**

## The Real Problem Wasn't Race—It Was Wealth

That moment forced me to see things differently. In South Africa, when people feel like they don't have enough, the easiest thing to do is **blame foreigners.**

*"They're taking our jobs."*
*"They're using up our resources."*
*"They're the problem."*

But here I was, in Germany, watching the **exact same pattern play out.**

The frustration of the poor was directed at migrants, at people who looked different, at outsiders, people who had no power —**not at the system that kept them poor in the first place.**

The truth was, that man wasn't angry at me. He was angry at his own situation. And when people are desperate, **they don't blame the system. They blame the people closest to them, who seem like easy targets.**

It wasn't a race issue. **It was a poverty issue disguised as a race issue.**

## What Germany Taught Me About Wealth

Before going to Germany, I thought wealth was just about having more money. As I stood in the **Mercedes-Benz Museum,** learning about how an entire industry was built from precision and long-term vision, I realized something deeper.

Wealth isn't just about **money.**

It's about **having the space to think beyond survival.** In South Africa, so many of us grow up in survival mode. We're constantly thinking about:

How do I afford school? How am I going to afford basic necessities? How do I get through this semester? How do I make rent this month? We don't get to ask bigger questions.

But in Germany, I saw what happened when **a society didn't have to fight for every little thing.** They could dream bigger. They could plan further ahead. They could build industries instead of just making it to the next paycheck.

And that's the real inequality. Not just **who has money and who doesn't**—but **who has the mental and emotional freedom to plan beyond tomorrow.**

## Taking the Lesson Home

Germany didn't have all the answers. Wealth inequality still existed. People still struggled. Even in one of the most structured, well-resourced countries in the world, **some people were still left behind.** But what I took from that trip was something deeper:

**Wealth isn't about how much you have—it's about what you're able to do with what you have.** And the real challenge isn't just giving people money.

It's creating a world where more people have the space to think, to dream, and to build beyond just survival. Because when that happens?

**That's when real change begins.**

## The Power of the People

That's what Wits gave me. Not just an education. Not just a degree. But a **new way of seeing the world.** It showed me that we were never meant to do this alone. That the greatest movements, the greatest ideas, the greatest revolutions—they never started with **individuals.** They started with **people who came together.**

When society learns how to move together—without needing people to think the same, without needing to agree on everything—**we become unstoppable.** What can **South Africa** achieve if we **harness that power?** If we **channel our energy**

**into something greater than ourselves?**

If we stop waiting for someone else to create change and realize that we are the ones we've been waiting for? Wits was a reminder. That power? **It has always belonged to the people.**

I walked into Wits alone, unsure of what I would become. I left knowing that I was part of something bigger. I left knowing that change was possible—not because of leaders or politicians, but because of ordinary people.

And when I stepped onto that graduation stage, I wasn't just celebrating a degree. I was carrying every lesson, every conversation, every fight, every sacrifice that had shaped me. I was carrying the proof of what happens when people **stand together**.

# 5

# Truth or Dare

Most parents don't want to hear that their child is starting an NGO instead of taking the safe route of a corporate graduate program. My parents, however, believed in me. That in itself was a luxury—one that so many young people don't have.

I remember the moment I told them—one of those pivotal moments where time slows down just enough for you to recognize that you're standing at a crossroads. If your dreams don't scare you, they aren't big enough.

For some reason, I thought my parents wouldn't approve, that they'd tell me to be realistic, to choose stability. Instead, they were **beaming with pride**.

I had just turned down a chance to enter one of South Africa's most prestigious quantitative finance programs—a direct line into banking, corporate power, and a salary that would make my financial struggles disappear. And for what?

**To build something from scratch. To register a nonprofit. To take a risk with no clear safety net. It sounded crazy. Maybe it was.**

But sometimes, *crazy* is just another word for vision.
And as much as this moment felt like a huge leap into the unknown, I wasn't actually unfamiliar with chaos. I had spent my entire life navigating a world that didn't quite make sense to me, constantly finding ways to adapt.

What I know until now is that the reason I was always writing things down in notepads wasn't just because I had too many ideas—it was a form of something called stimming.

Stimming, short for self-stimulatory behavior, is common in neurodivergent people, especially those with Autism and ADHD. It involves repetitive movements, sounds, or actions that help regulate emotions, focus, or process overwhelming sensations. Some people flap their hands, rock back and forth, or tap their feet. Me? I wrote.

I wrote everything. Lists, plans, thoughts, half-sentences that didn't make sense to anyone else, entire pages filled with the same word over and over again just because the motion of writing calmed my brain. My notebooks weren't just filled with ideas; they were filled with my way of making sense of the world.

Autism loved the **consistency** of a notepad and pen, always readily available. The structure of knowing I had a place to offload my thoughts gave me a sense of security in a world that often felt unpredictable. The feel of the paper, the familiar weight of the pen, the repetitive motion of writing—it was grounding. I never had to worry about my thoughts disappearing into a void. They were there, tangible, real and safe.

ADHD, on the other hand, thrived on the **novelty**. Attending conferences meant I was always collecting different notebooks and pens. Every event handed them out like candy, and unlike most people, I actually used them. A new notebook every week? Heaven. The fresh start, the crisp, untouched pages, the slightly different texture of the paper—little things that kept my brain engaged and interested.

Somehow, these two opposing needs—consistency and novelty—found harmony in something as simple as writing things down. Maybe that's why, to this day, I still prefer putting pen to paper. It's not just about capturing ideas. **It's about balance.** It's about movement. It's about finding a rhythm that works for me.

That's the thing about neurodivergent brains—what looks like quirks from the outside are actually essential survival mechanisms.

While my peers were familiarizing themselves with their new office spaces, I was familiarizing myself with bureaucratic red tape. I spent my days designing logos, studying SARS regulations, and navigating nonprofit compliance under the Department of Social Development.

**No one tells you how much paperwork goes into a dream.** I learned about tax exemptions, fundraising structures, and the complicated but necessary rules of engagement for running an organization in South Africa. Every step forward felt like three steps back.

## The Stability That Allowed for Chaos

If there's one thing that has made my journey with AuDHD manageable, it's stability at home. The chaos of my ambitions never had to fight for space with chaos in my personal life. Everything outside could be uncertain, overwhelming, and unpredictable—but inside my home? Nothing changed.

Mom still made her delicious chicken curries for Sunday lunch, no matter what was going on. My dad dropped and fetched me, making sure I got where I needed to be. My dog Momo still followed me around like a tiny, devoted tail, always ready to give me the best cuddles. I was always filling up notepads—pages overflowing with ideas, plans, and half-finished thoughts. My house was always littered with cups of cold tea and coffee that I had fully intended to drink but somehow never got to.

I still fought with my family to put the TV softer when they were watching action movies, only to turn around and scream at the TV with them during a Manchester United match. I still loved gardening, still loved arts and crafts, still asked too many questions, still spent hours on YouTube learning random facts, and still obsessively kept up with Duolingo, trying to learn every language under the sun.

Autistic people often rely on routines to create a sense of safety in a world that feels overwhelming. ADHD brains, on the other hand, crave novelty and excitement. My life has always been a contradiction between the two—needing structure but chasing the next big thing. The only reason I could pour all my energy into the uncertainty of building an NGO was because everything else in my life remained stable.

That's something many neurodivergent people don't get the privilege of.

## The Mind That Works Differently

At a WDB (Women's Development Bank) South Africa event—a powerful gathering of rural women, business leaders, and students—something clicked. An experience I hold in my heart quite fondly. I will never forget. I met Vhuthuhawe Mapholi.

She loves telling a very specific story about me.

During the Q&A session—sitting in a room full of some of the most powerful women in the country—I stood up, chest high, confidence unwavering, ready to drop what I thought was an absolute gem of an idea:

"Maybe instead of focusing solely on building more physical schools in rural areas, the government should invest in telecommunications infrastructure. E-learning could provide a practical solution for students who have to walk hours just to get to school."

The reaction?

Gasps. A few scandalized whispers. Side-eyes so intense they could have knocked me over. This was long before COVID made remote learning mainstream—back when the idea of e-learning as a primary mode of education sounded borderline absurd.

In hindsight? Maybe I was just ahead of the curve.

That's the thing with an AuDHD brain. It *sees the future* before everyone else does. It connects dots that others don't see yet. And sometimes, the way I process information doesn't align with how people *hear* things.

Vhuthu always says, *"Callan, you don't just think outside the box—you build a whole new one."*

Some ideas are ahead of their time. Some perspectives don't land the way you intend.

*But being misunderstood? That's practically a personality trait at this point.*

## Trusting the Right People

Nothing reveals people's true feelings about you like ambition. The moment I started reaching for something bigger than myself, some people disappeared. Not out of malice. Out of discomfort. I had to trust my gut and keep going—even when some of my university friends thought I was insane. But the thing about people doubting you?

It's fuel.

And I was ready to burn it.

The people you start a journey with aren't always the ones who will walk with you until the end. Success makes some people disappear—but it also makes room for the right ones to enter. And that's when I learned the biggest lesson of all.

When you move with purpose, the right people, opportunities, and resources align.

But first?

You must begin.

## Finding Mentors in Unexpected Places

Sometimes, the right people show up just when you need them. I still don't know what made me send that email. Maybe it was **naivety**, maybe **audacity**, or maybe I just didn't know enough to be afraid of rejection.

With nothing but a Facebook page, a dream, and what must have been a fascinating email to receive, I hustled my way on 702 Talk Radio, discussing my NGO, WakeUp ShakeUp SA. By "we," I mean me and my little dog, Momo.

It wasn't glamorous. It wasn't perfect. But it was real.

I had no corporate sponsors, no official backing—just **a belief that if the right people heard what we were trying to do, they would care**.

And somehow, it worked.

Yes, I ended up on **live radio**, talking about WakeUp ShakeUp SA—my voice steady, my words clear, as if I actually knew what I was doing. But here's the thing: you never know **who's listening**. And one of those listeners was **Derek**.

## The Mentor I Didn't See Coming

Derek was **not** the kind of person who handed out encouragement freely. If you came unprepared, if you hadn't done the work, if you were full of vague dreams with no concrete steps—he wouldn't entertain it. **He had no patience for empty ambition.**

But he also had **an eye for potential**.

Derek had spent years working in social development, understanding philanthropy not as an act of charity but as **a system**—one that required strategy, execution, and sustainability. And when he heard me on **702**, something must have **piqued his interest**. Maybe he thought I was crazy. Maybe he was **curious about this young woman who was bold enough to launch an NGO from scratch**.

Maybe he just wanted to see **if I was serious**. Whatever the reason, he reached out. At first, I wasn't sure **what to make of him**.

Derek could be **gruff**, **intimidating**, and **absolutely unforgiving** if he thought you weren't pulling your weight. But he also knew **how to get things done**. And unlike many people who nodded politely and wished me luck, **he actually helped**. He didn't mentor in the way most people imagine. He didn't hold my hand. He **opened doors**. He connected me to the **right people**, forced me to think **bigger**, and showed me that social impact wasn't about passion alone—it was about **positioning yourself until things worked**.

*"Things don't happen by accident, Callan. You position yourself until they do."*

That one sentence stayed with me. Because it was **true**. Derek passed away in **2024**, but his impact **remains**.

And what we built?

That was proof that he was right.

## Building the Young Women's Development Programme

Under Derek's mentorship, **we created the Young Women's Development Programme**—a series of workshops held in **Eldorado Park, Kagiso, and Chiawelo in Soweto**.

This wasn't some **feel-good event** where we gave speeches and left.

This was **real work**.

It was **structured**, **intentional**, and built to give young women **real, practical skills**—not just inspiration but the tools to **navigate a world that had never been designed for them to succeed**. It was about **self-discovery**, about breaking through the **mental barriers** that kept young women from seeing themselves as powerful, capable, and worthy of more. It was about **hard conversations**—about gender-based violence, workplace inequality, and the **reality** of being a woman in a country where safety was never guaranteed.

It was about **the future**—not just any future, but one where **young women had access to digital skills**, where they could step into industries dominated by men and **take up space with confidence**.

And it was about **community**—because no one rises alone. The women in those rooms were extraordinary. Some had already **raised siblings on their own**. Some had already **survived things that most people never recover from**. Some had already been told, over and over again, that they **would never amount to anything**.

But they were there.

They **showed up**.

And that alone was proof of their **resilience**.

## The Moment It Became Real

At one of our busiest events, we ran out of food. There were **so many women in the room** that we had to **stretch what we had**. Vhuthu, my mom, and I found ourselves cutting sausage rolls with a **plastic spoon**, making sure **everyone** got something to eat. And in that moment, as I looked around the room, I **felt it**.

This was real. This was **no longer just an idea**.

This thing—this wild, hyperfocused, hyperfixated AuDHD thought that had once existed **only in my mind**—had **materialized** into something people could touch, experience, and walk away from changed. I had taken something that was once just **scribbles in my notebook at 3 AM** and turned it into a room full of women who believed in themselves a little more than they did yesterday.

It wasn't just about **me** anymore.
It was **bigger than me**.
And **that** was victory.

## What I Know Until Now

At **Wits**, I learned **the theory**. At **WakeUp ShakeUp SA**, I learned the **practical**. Wits taught me about **inequality**, about **systems**, about **how power worked**.

But it wasn't until I stood in a room **full of women who had**

**never been given a fair chance** that I truly **understood** what it meant to **fight for something real.** Somewhere along the way, we were told that **change** comes from governments, from powerful institutions, from the hands of people who already have the world at their feet.

But that's a lie.

**Real change**—the kind that actually lasts—comes from **people who refuse to wait for permission**.

My parents knew this. Vhuthu knew this. Zanele Mbheki knew this. Derek knew this. The women in those rooms knew this.

And now, **I knew it too.**

6

# Feel The Need

By late 2019, I felt like I was pushing against a wall that refused to budge. I was pouring everything I had into my work, but it felt like the universe had other plans. It was like standing at the edge of something I couldn't yet see, sensing the shift before it arrived. My social development work was going nowhere. Funding requests that would have easily been approved in the past were now being rejected without explanation.

It didn't make sense. I had built successful programs with far less. The frustration sat heavy on my chest. It was as if the world was holding its breath, waiting for something.

I had no idea that something was a global pandemic. But before COVID changed everything, my own world had already shifted.

## My Grandmother's Business Was Love

My grandmother was my first and greatest business inspiration. She didn't have an MBA, a LinkedIn profile, or investment capital, but she understood something most business schools fail to teach: **feel the need and fulfill it.**

She knew what people wanted before they even did. Her Christmas cakes weren't just cakes; they were tradition, comfort, and joy. People didn't just buy them for December—they were ordering them for birthdays, for celebrations months down the line. Her mango atchar? It wasn't just a condiment—it was a taste of home, a piece of nostalgia, a staple in kitchens across the community.

She loved people, and they loved her back. That was her business model. And that, more than any strategy or revenue projection, is the real secret sauce.

She grew up in Nongoma, a town in KwaZulu-Natal, and was the granddaughter of an English grandfather and a Zulu grandmother—an interracial couple in a time when love like theirs was dangerous. Apartheid South Africa liked to paint the origins of Coloured people with one brushstroke, focusing only on the horrors of rape and forced relations. But what they tried to erase were the stories of **genuine love**—the ones that didn't fit their narrative of control.

Like many others, my family became a mix of cultures and identities that didn't neatly fit into a single box. Being Coloured in South Africa meant **belonging everywhere and nowhere at once.** It meant learning to adapt, to move between spaces, to

understand people at their core. And maybe that's why my grandmother was so good at business—because she **understood people.**
And at the end of the day, business is about people.

## The Business of Caring

She didn't just sell Christmas cakes and atchar. She sold warmth, care, and connection. And even now, when people ask me what my secret is—why my projects succeed, why my ideas work, why I always seem to know what's needed—I think about her.

I **feel the need,** and I give people **what they need.** Sometimes, it's tough love. Sometimes, it's the truth they don't want to hear. Sometimes, it's guidance, sometimes it's an opportunity. And sometimes, **it's just a hug.**

## A Loss That Shifted Everything

December 2019 changed my life. My grandmother—the only grandparent I had ever known—passed away. Her presence was a force, her wisdom a guiding light. With her passing, it felt as if a part of my foundation had been pulled from beneath me.
She was the strongest woman I had ever met, and with her went a history that I was still trying to piece together. In a strange way, I was grateful that she passed when she did. She left surrounded by family, with hands to hold, love in the room,

and the full rituals of mourning.

Just a few months later, those traditions would have been stripped away. COVID robbed so many of that final goodbye, forcing grief into isolation.

Grieving with AuDHD is its own kind of chaos. My brain didn't let me process it in the way people expect grief to look. Instead, **I hyperfixated on her life**—on every detail I could collect. I obsessed over making the perfect memorial video, carefully curating images, songs, and clips that captured her spirit. I poured over memories, dissecting the way she lived. And then, standing there at her funeral, giving my speech, it hit me.

**I was following in her footsteps.**

We had lived completely different lives, yet we had come to the same conclusions about life. Although she had never studied business, she had figured out what most CEOs never do: **Life is simple. We are the ones who over complicate it.**

Her legacy wasn't in what she built but in **how she made people feel.** And I realized that, even though I had the privilege of learning things she never had access to, everything I had learned validated what she had always taught me.

That's the thing about wisdom—it doesn't change, only the way it is delivered.

## The Lie of Individualism

For the first time in modern history, the world was forced to stop. **Not slow down—stop.** The streets emptied, businesses shuttered, and airports fell silent. And in that pause, **something unexpected happened.** For a brief moment, we were forced to see beyond ourselves.

The world had spent decades selling us the illusion of individualism—the idea that success is personal, that we are responsible only for ourselves, and that survival is a solo mission. But **COVID-19 shattered that illusion.** For the first time, we were all focused on the **collective.**

We realized that the actions of one could impact the lives of many. That a virus spreading in a market in Wuhan could shut down an entire planet. That the health of a street vendor in Johannesburg was tied to the health of an executive in London. We had always been intertwined. The pandemic just forced us to see it. And yet, as soon as the world began to reopen, some people rushed to forget. People wanted **"normal"** back. But **normal** had been broken long before COVID.

The cracks in our systems—the inequality, the exploitation, the deep fractures in how we valued life—had always been there. The pandemic didn't create them. It simply **exposed them.**

## What I Know Until Now

We make life unnecessarily hard. We chase things that don't matter. We complicate what should be simple. We ignore the needs of others and, in doing so, we ignore the needs within ourselves.

But **life is simple.**

**Feel the need.**

Then **do something about it.**

Sometimes, **you are the one in need.** Sometimes, the best thing you can do is **ask for what you need.** And sometimes, the best thing you can give **isn't money, or advice, or strategy.**

Sometimes, it's just **presence.** A **smile.** A **hug.** A reminder that **we're all in this together.**

# 7

# Touch The Sky

## Women Have Always Been Here

Women in tech. Women in AI. Women in leadership. We've heard the slogans, seen the panels, and attended the events. The hashtags trend, the photo ops circulate, and yet—**how much actually changes?**

The reality? Too many of these initiatives exist just for PR. They are neatly packaged displays of progress with very little action behind the scenes. I have watched as companies throw diversity events while continuing to overlook, underpay, and undervalue the women already working within their walls. I have watched as people applaud themselves for inclusion when, in reality, they're still gatekeeping the real opportunities.

But let's be clear: **women have always been here.**

Long before "women in STEM" became a marketing tool, before we had to fight for a seat at the table and demand recognition for our contributions, we were leading innovation. Women have been scientists, engineers, inventors, authors, and visionaries since the beginning of time. The only difference now is that **we have to fight twice as hard to be acknowledged.**

History is filled with brilliant women forced into the shadows. Female authors had to publish under male pseudonyms just to be taken seriously. Women in science saw their research stolen or attributed to male colleagues. Women who were told they didn't belong in the fields they pioneered helped shape the foundation of medicine, technology, and literature. The world has long benefitted from women's genius while refusing to give them credit.

**And still, we persist.**

## A Feminine Approach to AI

Women don't just solve problems; we anticipate them. We don't just build—we create ecosystems, filling the gaps that others overlook. We are the ones who ensure homes, communities, and businesses keep running. We pour our energy into our families, our societies, and our industries, often carrying the weight of a world that refuses to acknowledge just how much it relies on us.

That is exactly why a feminine approach to AI is not just necessary—it is long overdue. If women—across backgrounds, experiences, and industries—led the way in shaping AI, it wouldn't just be about representation. It would be about designing technology that serves everyone. AI would prioritize care over conquest, focusing on well-being rather than just productivity and profit. Systems would be built around ethics, fairness, and accountability—not because regulations demand it, but because we demand it. The best decisions wouldn't come from data alone but from an understanding of context, culture, and human emotion.

**The absence of diverse voices in AI doesn't just mean exclusion—it means flawed technology.** We have seen what happens when the same perspectives dominate: Systems fail to recognize darker skin tones, hiring algorithms discriminate, and healthcare AI misdiagnoses women because research is still largely based on male physiology. The consequences of exclusion are real. The question is, **when will we stop allowing it?**

## Equality Feels Like Oppression to Those Who Benefited from Inequality

When the status quo begins to shift, those who have long benefited from the imbalance call it unfair. We see this in boardrooms, in funding decisions, in the way women in leadership are scrutinized more harshly than their male counterparts.

But equity is not oppression. It is a correction. It is long overdue. And it is not just about doing what's right—it is about making better decisions, building better technology, and creating a future that **serves all of humanity,** not just a select few.

## The Woman Who Changed Everything: Lynda Marthinus

Some leaders don't just inspire you—they shake you awake. They refuse to accept mediocrity, push you past your comfort zone, and demand that you rise to the level they see in you before you even recognize it yourself. Lynda Marthinus was one of those people.

I met Lynda through the Innovator Trust, an organization investing in technology entrepreneurs. It was COVID times, and I had joined a virtual event hoping to see strong, hardcore women in the tech space. Instead, the panel was filled with powerful, inspiring women—but none of them were **truly in the trenches of the technology industry.**

Frustrated, young, bold, and maybe a little reckless, I took to Twitter and Instagram, tagging these leaders and asking the difficult questions about the lack of representation.

Lynda was the only person who responded. Her answer wasn't defensive or dismissive. She simply said, *"I don't know. Why don't we have a call to discuss it?"*

That was my first lesson from her: **Leadership isn't about having all the answers—it's about having the courage to find them.**

Lynda wasn't just a leader in the corporate sense—she was a force. As Vodacom's Executive Director for BEE and Transformation, she developed policies, negotiated groundbreaking deals, and invested in initiatives that shaped the landscape for Black and women-owned businesses. But beyond the titles and accolades, she was a woman who demanded excellence.

Her favorite lines in life were, ***"Never make excuses for being who you are,"*** **and** ***"Live your truth, be your authentic self."***

And so, you can only imagine the work she did with me. We fought—intensely. Sometimes, it felt like she was attacking me, pushing every insecurity, every doubt, every excuse I had ever made for myself. But I knew it came from love. She saw something in me before I did, and she wasn't going to let me hide from it.

Lynda beat cancer twice. When she was diagnosed a third time, she let me stay by her side in the early days. I prayed with her. I heard her wake up in the morning, blasting gospel music, singing loudly—ready for the fight ahead. If there was anyone who could beat cancer three times, it was her.

But she also knew I wasn't strong enough to fight this battle with her. Three months in, she asked me to leave and focus on my own life. **The strength of that decision still amazes me today.** She was fighting for her own survival, yet she was still looking out for me.

A few months later, I got the call I had been dreading. Holding her hand the day before she passed was surreal. But her legacy lived on. The fight for unity, peace, equality, justice, and prosperity didn't end with her. The day she passed, something shifted in me. I realized that every lesson, every push, every battle we fought together wasn't just about my success—it was about ensuring I carried the torch for others. Lynda was the force that made me step up, and now, I had to be that force for someone else.

## Touch the Sky: Entering the Big Leagues

My dad used to blast *"Touch the Sky"* before big soccer matches. During their warm-up, his boys moved in perfect unison. They looked like professional athletes, moved like a team, and trusted each other.

I was now in my own version of the big leagues.

I was sitting in rooms with the leaders you see in magazines, newspapers, and TV. I was learning how business leaders think. Executive thinking is something else. They are always thinking, always dreaming, constantly strategizing about their businesses, their people, and their industries—not just for today, but for the next five, ten, sometimes even twenty years. Just like my dad's soccer team relied on each other, women should be doing the same. We cannot afford to move alone. We must move like a team. Lynda changed my life. And I want to be that person for other women. For young girls who think they're too bold, too loud, too much. For women who have been doubted, overlooked, and underestimated. And even for the guys who want to be part of the solution.

Because at the end of the day, this is what community building looks like.

**No team wins when its players move in isolation. No movement succeeds without its members lifting each other up. And no industry will change if we keep pretending this is a women's fight alone. Equality is not a woman's burden to carry—it's everyone's responsibility.**

# 8

# Her Light

What started as a simple funding requirement from the Department of Social Development turned into an obsession. I began analyzing social development data, thinking it would just be a necessary administrative step, but before I knew it, **I was hooked**. The numbers weren't just statistics; they were stories. They spoke of hidden realities in communities like Eldorado Park, Alexandra, and Kagiso, bringing to life struggles that were both **fascinating and heartbreaking**.

Through the data, I saw the different battles people were fighting. Unemployment in Eldorado Park and Alexandra wasn't just about the lack of jobs—it was a complex weave of skill gaps, bravado, drug abuse, and miseducation. Kagiso, on the other hand, had a different struggle: infrastructure. Unlike Alexandra, which sat right next to Sandton, or Eldorado Park, just a 30-minute drive from Johannesburg's economic hub, Kagiso was trapped by distance. It could take up to two hours to reach the city during peak traffic. Imagine spending most of your income just to get to a job interview—assuming you could even afford the trip. **Discouragement would be understandable.** A lack of transport networks, unreliable roads, no viable train system—economic mobility was impossible when the very infrastructure meant to support movement didn't exist.

This was when I fell in love with data. Numbers didn't just sit there—they spoke. They told stories of hardship, inequality, and systems that weren't designed for everyone. And, as luck would have it, I had the right background to do something about it. The problem? At the time, nobody really knew what a "data scientist" was. The concept of hiring someone to extract insights from data was still a foreign idea to most companies, and opportunities were few and far between.

## Pi Day and the Wake-Up Call

While I was deep in my data science hyperfixation, I was also planning an event for WakeUp ShakeUp SA. I had this brilliant idea to celebrate Pi Day on March 14th by handing out mini pies and teaching kids about STEM careers and the importance of pure mathematics. I've always believed that math should be taught like a language—because, really, it is. Arithmetic is just grammar. Imagine only learning grammar but never getting to express yourself in the language you're speaking? That's how most people experience math. **People don't realize how creative and expressive math can be.**

But while I was lost in the numbers, I lost track of my daily bread. I had been so deep in my newfound love for data science and AI that I forgot about actually keeping the NGO running. Funding for Pi Day was suddenly pulled, and I found myself struggling financially—again.

## A Strange Detour: High-Performance Computing

Before I go on, let me tell you a ridiculous story. Back at university, I was minding my own business in the computer science labs, working on math optimization homework, when one of my many eccentric friends shouted, "Hey Cal, join our Supercomputing team! Apparently, we need a girl! Oh, and don't you want to be our leader?"
I laughed, thinking it was a joke. Naturally, I responded, "Oh yes, of course, sounds great!"—full sarcasm.

**It was not a joke.**

A few months later, I found myself at Kruger National Park, competing in a High-Performance Computing (HPC) competition. One thing about me? I'm extremely competitive. We came in third place, which I contested because our team was more affected by "load shedding" than the others because of the very innovative and creative way that we decided to build our solution. But the real lesson? Sometimes you take a risk, and it doesn't work out. Also, Kruger Park? A terrible place for an HPC competition. To the organizers: we listen, we don't judge.

But what I did take away from that experience were unknowingly skills that would also help me excel at data science later in life. Once I realized this, my curiosity turned into an all-consuming mission. I barely slept. I spent weeks, months—**diving deep into data science, AI, and the future of technology.** Every waking moment was dedicated to understanding, experimenting, and refining my knowledge. What started as an interest became an unstoppable drive, a need to unravel every detail and predict where the world was heading.

## The Hard Reality: Struggle Was Back

At the same time, I was still paying my bills with math tutoring and my small NGO salary. I was barely keeping my head above water when funding was dropped for Pi Day.

With my finances crumbling and my mental health hanging by a thread, reality hit hard. Running an NGO wasn't sustainable. I wasn't growing, I was barely surviving, and I had to pivot. The problem was, **I felt guilty**.

Then, one day at one of our Women's Development Programme events, someone pulled me aside. They told me I looked awful—exhausted, drained, sickly. My spark was gone. My eyes had dark circles. It was too much.

In hindsight, I now realize that on-the-ground NGO work is incredibly overstimulating for someone who has AuDHD, and if I ever did this kind of work again, it would need to be as part of a larger community effort, not just me taking everything on alone. My sensory system was completely overwhelmed, and I was feeling the consequences. My burnout was real—not just physical exhaustion, but emotional burnout too. As much as I was giving my life to this cause, things weren't getting any better. The weight of seeing the same struggles repeat themselves, despite all my efforts, was crushing.

The data showed me that something needed to be done at a

larger scale. I had to pivot, not just for myself but to create real, lasting change that could actually make a difference.

## Unemployment Will Break You

Pivoting wasn't easy. I knew I needed a new job, but for three months, absolutely nothing happened. I applied for positions, sent emails, networked—and nothing. **Silence**.

I went from constant chaos to hearing nothing at all, and it drove me insane. Unemployment is more than just financial stress—it destroys your sense of self-worth. I only had to endure three months, but most people in South Africa **endure years, even decades.** This is why I'm passionate about solving youth unemployment. The experience changes you.

This is also why I take a **human-centric approach to AI.** The groundbreaking technology of artificial intelligence should be used to empower people, not replace them. I believe artificial intelligence has the power to remind us what being human is all about. We don't need to live like robots when we have ***actual*** robots.

We should be building Iron Man suits—giving people superhuman abilities—not Terminator-type AI that wipes people out and adds nothing to the economy. Replacing human workers entirely with AI isn't just unethical—it's counterproductive. Machines cannot replicate human creativity, emotional intelligence, and adaptability. Societies thrive when technology enhances productivity and empowers people, not when it replaces livelihoods and deepens inequality. The most successful innovations throughout history have amplified human potential rather than rendering people obsolete.

## Surviving Unemployment: Giving Myself a Job

I had to crawl my way out of the dark mental space unemployment created. I started waking up early, and I gave myself a job.

I took a hardened piece of ground in our yard and worked 9-5 every day to turn it into a garden. I made my own compost and grew tomatoes, bell peppers, and even butternut from the seeds of our kitchen scraps.

One day, one of my mom's friends felt sorry for me and split her agapanthus so I could plant it in my new little garden. At the time, that was the nicest thing anyone could have done for me. **To this day, I love agapanthus—they've become a symbol of hope and resilience for me, a reminder that even in the hardest moments, growth is possible**.

Well, except for maybe sending me an email that said, "You got the job." Ironically, that happened on the same day.

There's a lesson in that. Keeping your mind active and positive matters. You have to direct your energy somewhere, or your brain will do whatever it wants.

I finally got my first real data science job at a consulting company. I also received offers for tech consulting work, but I put them on hold to give this new role my all.

**It wasn't great.**

I experienced a lot of discrimination and absolute madness in my first job. To this day, I can't believe that I survived what I went through while working at my first Data-Science job. The leadership? They'd probably be in prison today if I had evidence of what they did. I could tell you but, I don't think you'd believe me. And so let that be a story for another day.

As much as I went through absolute hell at my first job, I was grateful for the stepping stone. No matter how bad it was, it was still better than being unemployed. It was the start of my new journey. And recently, in 2025, I had a full-circle moment—meeting people from the United Nations' World Food Organization. I had the opportunity to speak to them about **AI use cases that could change the game** for them.

From analyzing poverty statistics to helping global organizations understand how AI could transform food security, pivoting was proof that it had been the right decision.

This was just the beginning of something bigger.

**What I Know Until Now is that passion is not enough. Real change requires strategy, adaptability, and knowing when to pivot.**

At Wits, I learned the theory. At WakeUp ShakeUp SA, I learned the practical. Data had led me here. The numbers had shown me where the real problems were. And instead of resisting, I listened.

**Success isn't just about hard work.**

**It's about knowing when to pivot.**

# 9

# Samba Pa Ti

## The Art of Having Everything and Feeling Nothing

On the surface, I was living my best life. A well-paying job in machine learning at a multinational. Weekends filled with fancy restaurants, spa days, and those local trips that only tourists usually get to enjoy. I explored the breathtaking beaches of Cape Town, marveled at the Drakensberg mountains, and indulged in wine tastings in Stellenbosch. I took in the energy of Maboneng in Johannesburg, visited the wildlife of Kruger National Park, and even experienced the cultural richness of places like Robben Island and Soweto.

South Africa had so much to offer, and I was determined to soak in every bit of it.

I spoiled myself, and I did it well. **Anything baby wanted, baby**

**got.**

The seafood at the V&A Waterfront was *so* fresh I was convinced it had been swimming just moments before it landed on my plate. The Drakensberg mist made me feel like I had stepped into a fantasy novel. The Stellenbosch wine tastings? I couldn't tell a Merlot from a Cabernet to save my life, but I nodded along like a seasoned sommelier.

But it wasn't about material things. I've never been one for flashy brands, but experiences? **That was my thing.**

I learned how to dance ballroom, I threw myself into new hobbies, I traveled, and I even took proper swimming lessons. It wasn't something I had ever prioritized, but one day, I decided—why not? Learning to swim as an adult felt both ridiculous and liberating, like I was undoing an entire childhood of avoiding the deep end.

For many people, swimming is just a casual life skill picked up in childhood, but for me, it was a milestone—a challenge accepted. There was something almost rebellious about standing in a pool, awkwardly trying to float while tiny children swam circles around me, completely unimpressed by my existential crisis. But I refused to be defeated by a body of water.
The first few lessons were humbling. Floating felt unnatural, kicking felt uncoordinated, and my breathing? A disaster. I spent more time inhaling water than actually swimming. But with each lesson, I started to feel more at ease. It wasn't just about learning how to swim; **it was about refusing to let life keep me in the shallow end.**

It reminded me of how some South Africans feel about finally getting their driver's license. For those who grow up with access to cars, it's just another step in life. But for many who rely on public transport, finally being able to drive represents a kind of independence and freedom that was previously out of reach. **Learning to swim gave me that same feeling—like I had unlocked something that should have been mine all along.**
But in between the luxurious meals, the polished work presentations, and the carefully curated moments of self-care, there was something else—something I couldn't quite name yet. A whisper beneath the surface, asking, **Is this it?**

## Success Without Purpose Is Just Performance

I was making the kind of money I never thought possible for myself growing up. The kind of money that, at one point, would have solved every problem I ever had. And yet, when I finally got there, it didn't feel like the answer.

I had reached the point where **success** was no longer about getting through the door. **It was about figuring out what the hell I was doing here.**

It was an odd kind of loneliness, one that doesn't come from the absence of people but from the absence of connection—to myself, to something greater. I had everything I was supposed to want, but something inside me was restless, like I was waiting for the next clue in a puzzle I didn't know I was solving.
At work, I was excelling. Machine learning was fascinating, and I was good at it. But the more I immersed myself in algorithms

and models, the more I realized something: **I wasn't in love with the work—I was in love with what the work could do.**

I started to see technology not just as a tool but as something bigger. It wasn't about building better models, it was about solving real-world problems, making systems smarter, and maybe even making the world a little more fair. The way machine learning could be applied to justice, accessibility, decision-making—it fascinated me.

Looking back, I see now that this was the beginning of something. A slow shift. A recognition that while success looked good on the outside, **purpose was the only thing that would ever feel right on the inside.**

## Burnout, Boredom, and the Breaking Point

I burned out.

Not from overwork, but from something far worse—**boredom.** Understimulation. Everything I had been through in my life had built resilience, but nothing prepared me for how dangerous boredom could be for someone like me.
Burnout isn't just exhaustion. **It's forgetting who you are outside of work.**

AuDHD is a constant balancing act between being under and over-stimulated, but for me, under stimulation was the real killer. I learned the hard way that I could never survive a normal, monotonous 9-5 job. It would drain the life out of me.

I kept convincing myself that I just needed to push through. But the exhaustion wasn't just in my head—it was in my body. When I finally collapsed, I learned the hard way that burnout doesn't just make you tired. **It breaks you.**

Burnout from boredom sent me to the hospital for exhaustion. You'd think they would diagnose me on the spot, but they didn't. Doctors never really listened long enough. Nothing was technically wrong, yet everything was wrong.

I wasn't depressed—I was AuDHD and under stimulated.

I wasn't anxious—I was AuDHD and overstimulated. But no one connected the dots.

I kept trying to push through, convincing myself that I was just ungrateful, just spoiled, just lazy. **How could I possibly feel this way when I had everything?**

## Finally Being Heard

No one listened long enough. Until Michelle Koen.

The sweetest therapist ever. She sat through all my chaotic, nonsensical stories, and for the first time, **someone actually heard me.** She introduced me to the term **AuDHD** at 30 years old, and suddenly, everything clicked.

For most of my life, I thought Autism and ADHD were "white

people things"—reserved for the Jono's in Bryanston. It never occurred to me that a South African Coloured woman like me could have it.

The realization came with an overwhelming mix of emotions—**relief, grief, and anger.**

*How had I gone three decades without knowing? How many times had I blamed myself for something that wasn't my fault? How different could my life have been if I had known earlier?*

In the famous words of South Africa's favourite pop-piano princess Tyla: **"What the Heck!"**

## Who Am I Without Achievement?

I had worked so hard to get here, to arrive at this version of myself that was accomplished and thriving. But I hadn't stopped to ask myself: **Who am I outside of achievement? Outside of ambition?**

I had spent years chasing success, chasing validation, chasing something that always seemed just out of reach. But now, for the first time, I wasn't chasing anything.

**I was standing still.**
**And I had no idea what that meant.**

# 10

# Vienna

Hindsight is everything. Looking back now, I realize just how much I could have done differently if I had known about my AuDHD. If I had understood why my brain works the way it does—why my energy fluctuates between unstoppable momentum and complete shutdown, why I hyperfixated on things that no one else seemed to grasp, why I could see things so clearly that others struggled to understand. This is why knowing matters. It's not about making excuses—it's about navigating life in a way that doesn't burn me to the ground. Starting **Data-Led Insights (DLI)** felt like stepping into a world where I could finally move at my own speed—fast, relentless, and driven. I had a vision, the skill, and the hunger to build something revolutionary. But I didn't know then that speed without endurance leads to burnout.

I ran DLI on pure momentum. My brain moved at lightning speed, solving data problems effortlessly, strategizing like a chess master, and spotting gaps in the market before most people even knew they existed. And for a while, it worked.

**DLI was thriving.**

We were doing something big, something meaningful. There was energy in the air every day—excitement, passion, the thrill of creating something from nothing. Late nights turned into early mornings, fueled by drive, purpose, and way too much KFC.

My best friend, **Vhuthuhawe Mapholi**, had just finished her articles and came to work with me. She was my ride-or-die, my mirror, the one person who could call me out when I was being unrealistic but would still stand by my side through everything. My brother **Jared**, having transitioned from his football career, was building a life for his family and his community. Steady, loyal, and newly married, he was my rock. The three of us, plus the growing DLI team, felt unstoppable.

## The Reality of Entrepreneurship

Entrepreneurship is a paradox. You build something to make life better—for customers, employees, even yourself. But as the founder, you're often the one who sacrifices the most. You go the extra mile, ensure everything runs smoothly, keep the vision alive—and yet, when things fall apart, you take the hardest hit.

It's easy to romanticize entrepreneurship. People love the success stories, the breakthrough moments, the celebrations. But what they don't tell you is that before those moments, there's struggle. There's exhaustion. There's standing at the edge of financial ruin, wondering if this is the moment it all collapses.

Building a business isn't just about having a vision. It's about survival. It's about navigating an unforgiving landscape where passion alone isn't enough. It's about making the hard decisions before the universe makes them for you.

I wasn't naive about my skills. I knew I was one of the best in my field. But I was naive about **the realities of running a business in South Africa**—a country where small businesses don't just compete with each other; they compete against a system designed to move too slow.

South African businesses don't fail because they lack talent or good ideas. They fail because contracts take too long, payments take even longer, and cash flow is king. When you're a small business, delays don't just mean inconvenience—they mean disaster.

And then there was the biggest lesson of all: **hiring the wrong people can destroy everything you built.**

## Trusting the Wrong People

At first, I thought I was making the right hiring decisions. I surrounded myself with people who seemed capable, who talked a big game, who convinced me they could help scale my vision. But what I learned the hard way is that not everyone is who they claim to be.

Some people saw DLI as an opportunity—not to grow, not to build, but to **take.**

I trusted the wrong people with too much control, and they **ran my business into the ground.** They mismanaged operations, created internal chaos, and ultimately left behind a mess I couldn't clean up fast enough.

The worst part? By the time I fully grasped what was happening, it was too late. And I had no one to blame but myself.

## The Debt, The Fall, and Retrenching Myself

When the walls started closing in, and the numbers weren't adding up, I did something I never thought I'd have to do—**I retrenched myself.**

It wasn't just about pride. It wasn't even just about the business. It was about **survival.**

I was sitting at my desk, staring at the cold, hard facts. The cash flow had dried up, the contracts were delayed, and the expenses weren't waiting for me to figure things out. The payroll had already been cut, the team had been let go, and there was no one left to sacrifice but me.

The idea felt absurd. How do you retrench yourself from your own company? How do you cut yourself out of something you built? But the truth was, if I didn't, **I was going to lose everything.** I wasn't just fighting to keep a business alive anymore. I was fighting to keep my home.

The bank doesn't care about your entrepreneurial dreams. The bank doesn't care that your contracts are delayed. The bank cares about **payments.**

I needed time. So I made a decision. **I stopped taking a salary.** I cut every expense that wasn't essential. I did everything I could to buy myself a few more months to keep the bank from knocking on my door.

Retrenching myself felt like failure. But looking back, I see it for what it really was: **strategy.**

## Vienna Waits for You

South Africans often box themselves in, thinking their market is only what's in front of them. But the truth is, **the world is bigger than South Africa.**

My mistake was depending too much on local contracts. Things moved way too excruciatingly slow, and I couldn't afford to wait. **So, I looked beyond South Africa.**

I started using LinkedIn and other online platforms to connect with European companies that needed my expertise. And suddenly, I had access to a **completely different market.** A market where payments were on time, contracts weren't delayed for months, and my skills were valued without hesitation.

Vienna was waiting.

Europe was waiting.
**The world was waiting.**

South African entrepreneurs don't have to limit themselves to South Africa. **Your customers aren't just here.** If you have a skill, a product, or a service, **take it global.**

And then? Bring what you learn back home.

## Back to Basics: The Comeback

Here's what I realized—**I didn't need a company to provide my services.** I built DLI, but at its core, my business was **me.** My knowledge, my skills, my ability to **see what others don't.** I didn't have to wait for the perfect moment to rebuild. I just had to **start again.**

Sometimes, to move forward, you have to go backwards. So, I went back to **being self-employed rather than an entrepreneur.** Instead of managing a company, I focused on doing the work myself. One contract at a time. One client at a time.

The debt was still there, but it wasn't the end of my story. This wasn't a loss.
**It was a reset.**

I didn't need a company to define me. I didn't need a brand to validate my expertise. In fact now I could focus on mastery of my skills. I had something more valuable—**experience, knowledge, and the ability to rebuild from nothing.**

And I did.

With **one client.** Then another. And another. Before I knew it, I had built something new.

DLI wasn't gone. **It had evolved.**

And so had I.

# 11

# Don't you worry 'bout a thing

Living in South Africa is an extreme sport. Every day comes with a new challenge, a new inconvenience, a new test of patience.

One minute, it's 5 AM, you're minding your business, making early morning breakfast, and the next—*boom*—load shedding. Now you're in the dark, boiling water on a gas stove like you're camping in your own house. You finally get the power back, and then you realize—no water. No warning, no explanation, just a casual reminder that basic services are a luxury, not a right.

And that's just *Monday morning*.

By the time you get to Friday, there's been another scandal, another corruption case, another viral moment that would shock any other nation but barely phases us anymore.

**It's a lot. And yet, despite it all, we move . We adjust. We keep going.**

But let's be honest—living in survival mode takes a toll. It messes with your nervous system, keeping you in a constant state of stress. And for someone like me, whose nervous system was already working overtime, it made everything ten times worse.

## The Silent Burden of Sensory Anxiety

For thirty years, I carried anxiety, not knowing what was wrong. My shoulders were always tense, my jaw clenched, my thoughts racing. It was like my body was permanently on high alert, bracing for impact.

I wish I had known sooner that it was the lights. That my brain was processing everything at a level most people couldn't even comprehend.

My dad would be watching football late at night, barely raising the volume, and I'd hear *everything*—the shuffle of him reaching for his drink, the movement of the ball, the commentator's voice, the sound of the couch cushions shifting under his weight.

"Callan, you have supersonic hearing," my family would joke.
**Hilarious.**

Except it wasn't so funny when I hadn't slept in three days because my brain refused to shut down.

I spent years doubting myself, wondering if I was overreacting, too sensitive, too dramatic. Turns out, I was just wired differently.

## The Worst Advice You Can Give an Anxious Person

Telling someone with anxiety to "just relax" is like telling someone drowning to "just swim."

You might as well punch me in the face. It's not about choice. It's not about effort. It's about the way your body and brain react to the world.

But what does help? Practical tools. Hacks. Distractions that *actually* work. Like carrying a packet of salt. The intense taste can snap your brain out of a panic attack. It sounds ridiculous, but it works. Sensory redirection is a game-changer.

Some people use ice cubes. Some splash cold water on their face. Some grip something textured to bring themselves back into their body. The trick isn't to fight the anxiety—it's to *outsmart* it.

And when it comes to stress? South Africa has its own version of outsmarting it.

## South Africa: The Class Clown of the World

You know how every school had a Grade 12C? The naughty class. The one full of jokers who never took anything seriously but somehow still made it through.

**That's South Africa.**

No matter what happens, we laugh. Maybe it's a defense mechanism. Maybe it's just how we survive.

Think about it—where else would a country turn a global health crisis into a comedy special? Remember **Polony-Gate**? The time processed meat nearly took us all out? A *police station* **got robbed**. Let that sink in—the place where criminals are *arrested* got *robbed.* And what about poor Uncle Cyril? He put on a mask awkwardly ONCE, and we never let it go. He misplaced his iPad, and now we even call our president ''*Cupcake*''.

We joke about it, we laugh about it, but is it because we don't take anything seriously?

Or are we afraid that if we stop laughing, **we'll start crying?**

## The Grief Cycle of a Nation

Denial. Anger. Bargaining. Depression. Acceptance.

That's the grief cycle. And if you watch South Africa long enough, you'll notice—we follow it exactly.

Denial: "Nah, this isn't happening."

Anger: "This is nonsense! How could they let this happen?"

Bargaining: "Maybe if we vote differently next time, things will change."

Depression: "Eish. Nothing's ever going to get better, hey."

Acceptance: "At least we still have pap and wors."

And then? We start the cycle all over again. Humor is how we cope, but at what point do we stop laughing and start demanding better?

## When Corruption Makes You Physically Sick

I don't mean that figuratively. I mean *actually* sick.

There's something about seeing the dreams of a nation traded for houses, cars, and foreign trips that makes me want to throw up. All those lives sacrificed for freedom, and for what? To line a politician's pockets? **But here's what keeps me hopeful—our democracy is *still young*.**

South Africa is only thirty years old. I am only thirty years old. We are growing together, stumbling together, figuring things out in real time. And when you really take a moment to look at it, **we *have* come far.**

## We Don't Always See the Change While It's Happening

The song says, *"You're the only one who sees yourself through the changes."* South Africa is changing. We just don't always recognize it. We hosted a World Cup. The Springboks are world champions. Even Bafana Bafana is giving us hope again.

We are still here. Still fighting. Still pushing forward.

The hope of a nation doesn't live in the hands of politicians—it lives inside each and every one of us.

**So let's not worry about a thing.**

If we *really* want a better country, we have to believe in it first. We have to believe in the good hearts and minds of the South African people. We have to believe that change is possible. We have to believe that things can get better, not just for ourselves but for everyone. We have to stop waiting for someone else to fix it and start fixing what we can, in our own way, wherever we are.

There's a African proverb that says: ***"If you want to go fast, go alone. If you want to go far, go together."***

South Africa is going far.

And **we are going together.**

# 12

# Becoming

I didn't wake up one day and decide to become a different person. Growth isn't that simple. It doesn't come in one single, earth-shattering realization where everything clicks into place. It comes in the small, difficult choices—the moments where you decide, over and over again, to show up for yourself, even when it **feels impossible.**

I used to believe that change would come in a grand, dramatic transformation. That one day, I'd have some kind of breakthrough, and suddenly, everything would be different. But real change doesn't happen like that. It happens in the quiet moments. In the decision to take care of yourself when no one is watching. In choosing to leave the spaces that no longer serve you. In walking away from people who drain you, even when it's painful. I realize that growth means **choosing yourself, even when it disappoints others.**

There were times when I felt like I was sprinting through life, chasing something just out of reach. I was always in motion, always trying to get to the next thing, always pushing myself past the point of exhaustion. I thought that was what success required, but that was the price I had to pay. But **burnout is not a badge of honor.** Success is meaningless if you destroy yourself trying to achieve it.

I had to learn to slow down. I want to listen to my body, honor my energy, and recognize that **rest is productive.** To accept that I couldn't keep moving at an unsustainable pace and expect to thrive.

For the longest time, I was terrified of failure. I thought failing meant I wasn't good enough, that I wasn't smart enough, that I wasn't worthy of the dreams I had for myself. But what I know now is that failure is **not the opposite of success—it's a necessary part of it.** Failure is how you learn. Failure is how you get stronger. Failure is how you grow.

What happened at DLI felt like the biggest failure of my life. It broke me in ways I didn't think I could recover from. But looking back, I can see that it was about transformation. It forced me to re-evaluate everything. To let go of things I had been holding onto too tightly. To strip away all the noise and get back to the core of who I really am.

## Rebuilding with My Brother

My brother, Jared, was also rebuilding. His football career was over, and instead of letting the transition break him, he channeled his energy into financial planning, specifically for athletes. He saw the cycle—athletes who make it big, spend recklessly, and then lose everything once their sports career ends. He wanted to change that.

Watching Jared rebuild gave me courage. It reminded me that starting over doesn't mean starting from scratch. **It means starting with experience, wisdom, and the hard-earned lessons that failure teaches you.**

And I realized how important siblings are to our life journeys. They see you at your best, at your worst, and every version in between. And sometimes, just seeing them move forward is enough to remind you that you can, too.

## Rising from the Ashes

Somehow, I rebuilt. It took relentless work—grinding every single day, figuring things out one step at a time. **Working until 2 a.m. became my norm.** There were no shortcuts, no lucky breaks—just persistence, late nights, and the unwavering belief that I could pull myself out of the mess.

I learned that discipline is an act of self-love—the most profound kind. It isn't about punishment or restriction; it's about choosing yourself, over and over again, even when the results aren't immediate. It's about making deposits into your future self's success, no matter how small. The effort I put in, the hours I dedicated, weren't just about getting ahead; they were about proving to myself that I had the power to rebuild, to transform, to rise. **Hard work wasn't just about success—it was about self-respect.**

And I did rise. Like a phoenix from the ashes.

## Sema Tawy

Ancient wisdom has echoed these sentiments for centuries. The Kemetic principle of Sema Tawy, meaning "the union of the two lands," represents balancing discipline and passion—**the merging of what you must do with what you love to do.** The most successful civilizations, warriors, and thinkers across history have always known that consistent effort and self-mastery are the keys to transformation.

Whether in ancient Egypt, where pharaohs built legacies stone by stone, or in modern times, where greatness is forged through grit, the message remains the same: nothing meaningful is built without work.

I threw myself into AI and consulting—my lifeline. It was the only thing that made sense, the only thing that brought me joy. Public speaking became another outlet and an income stream that I took seriously. Bit by bit, **I climbed out of the darkness.**

Financially, I recovered. Career-wise, I was thriving again.

But personally? I was still struggling. Nothing was over, not really. The struggle for balance, for purpose, for healing—it wasn't something that could be neatly wrapped up and left in the past. It was ongoing. But for the first time in a long time, **I was moving forward.**

I have always been someone who feels deeply. Someone who cares too much, who tries too hard, who gives more than she has. And for a long time, I thought that was a weakness. But I know now that it's my greatest strength. **The world doesn't need more people who are indifferent. It needs more people who care.**

I used to think I had to prove myself. That I had to justify my existence, my choices, my success. But I don't have to prove anything to anyone. I am not here to meet anyone's expectations. I am not here to fit into someone else's definition of success. **I am here to live fully, unapologetically, and on my own terms.**

The journey of becoming is not about arriving at some perfect destination where everything makes sense. It's about learning to be okay with the uncertainty. It's about trusting yourself enough to know that even when things fall apart, you will rebuild. Even when you don't have all the answers, you will figure it out. Even when the path is unclear, you will find your way.

So if you're in a place where you feel lost, if you're questioning everything, if you're wondering whether you'll ever get to where you want to be—**keep going.** Keep choosing yourself. Keep showing up. Keep becoming.

Because the truth is, **there is no final version of you.** You will always be growing, evolving, changing. And that's not something to fear—that's something to embrace.

And right now, in this moment, **I love who I'm becoming.**

# 13

# Table For Three

## The Most Important Decision You Will Ever Make

People don't realize that romantic relationships are the single most important decision you will make in your life. More than your career, more than where you live—your partner will affect your mental health, your physical health, your financial health, and your overall sense of self.

A bad partner can drain you, stunt your growth, or even ruin you completely. A good partner, however, can be a source of peace, strength, and support. I grew up with parents who had a loving relationship. My father is a gentleman, a protector, a provider, a quiet, steady man. Of course, I was never attracted to "bad boys." I never romanticized chaos. I wasn't drawn to dysfunction. No, I liked sweet, reliable, kind, trustworthy men. I've only ever been in two serious relationships, and even though both of those men were exactly that—sweet, loving, kind—it still didn't mean they were the right ones for me.

## The Relationship That Made Sense

Welden was my friend before he became my boyfriend. We dated for three years, and as it often happens, the natural societal expectation was marriage.

But he reminded me that it wasn't a great idea. He told me he couldn't marry me.

**Thank God**.

Welden was a real friend in that moment because if we had gone through with it, it would have been a marriage of convenience, not love. We were two emotionally unavailable people just ''Vibing''. We got along, we cared for each other deeply, but I think we both knew deep down that it wasn't the right fit. I'm grateful for his honesty because it saved both of us from making a life-altering mistake.

## The One That Came Close

With Kgabi, it was different. He saw me in a way that felt real, deep, and unshaken by the chaos of life. But I was even more emotionally unavailable when we met. I had trust issues after the fallout with certain individuals from DLI, and even though he supported and loved me through it, I couldn't let him in.

I was too busy trying to fix myself, too busy working on my businesses and my NGO, **too busy doing things for everyone else.**

Then, just as I started healing, just as I was beginning to open up and be present in the relationship, life took an unexpected turn.

His sister, Bonnie, **passed away suddenly.**

It was one of those deaths that shouldn't have happened. Unknown causes. **A failure of South Africa's broken healthcare system.**

Bonnie collapsed in her apartment, and by the time emergency services responded, she was gone. **Just like that.** She was brilliant, ambitious, one of the first Black female attorneys at an international law firm in Sandton. A rising star, a force of nature. And then, in an instant, she was gone.

**Her death changed everything.**

I watched as grief took over his entire being. He shut down. He withdrew from the world, from himself, from me. He had always been my rock, but now, he was the one sinking.

I did what I could to support his family, these were people **I cared about deeply**. I even cooked a few meals in their home, trying to bring comfort to a household drowning in sorrow. Making his mother smile—if even just for a second—felt like the only thing I could do.

**But it wasn't enough.**

Grief changes people. It reshapes them in ways that love alone cannot undo.

And just like that, **I lost him too.**

## Healing and Taking a Pause

That's when I realized something. I had been working on myself so hard, trying to fix what wasn't broken. I had been chasing, building, proving. But I had never actually paused to *be*.

**So I took a pause.**

**I re-evaluated.**

I recognized that I had time. I didn't have to rush into another relationship. I didn't have to seek love in another person.

I was okay on my own.

**I was whole on my own.**

There were already so many people in my life who loved me—my family, my friends, my community. I didn't need to rush into a partnership just because the world told me I should. I found joy in watching my niece and nephew grow up. I spent more time with the people who had always been there for me; my family. I learned to truly enjoy my own company.

## The Beauty of Being Alone

There's something powerful about enjoying your own company. About being able to sit with yourself, in silence, without seeking distraction or validation.

I started taking myself out to dinner, watching sunsets alone, traveling without the need for someone beside me. I listened to music that made me feel something. I bought myself flowers. I reminded myself daily: **I am enough.**

And the song that kept playing in my head?

**"One ain't gotta be a lonely number."**

## Me, Myself, and a Table for Three

*"Can I give me a moment, a second of my time?"*

*"Can I take my mind and place my attention on me only?"*

I wasn't waiting for anyone to show up and make me feel special. I was giving that to myself. I used to think self-love was just a cliché, something people said but didn't really mean. But now, I get it. It's not about spa days or face masks or feel-good Instagram quotes. It's about **showing up for yourself** the way you wish someone else would.

It's about becoming your own safe space. It's about knowing

that **love starts with you.** I don't know what the future holds for me in terms of relationships. But what I do know is that I will never again seek love from a place of lack.

I am already full.

I am already whole.

And this one is **not** a lonely number.

# 14

# Energy

## Creating and Cultivating Energy

Attention dear reader! Please don't check out of this one just because it sounds like a 'wellness' topic. You need to know this. We all do. Because if there's one thing I've learned, it's that success isn't just about talent, strategy, or even hard work. **It's about energy**. The ability to create it, sustain it, and cultivate it—not just for yourself, but for others.

The people who seem unstoppable? It's not because they never get tired, never struggle, or never doubt themselves. It's because they've mastered how to manage their energy. They know when to go full speed and when to pull back. They understand that real progress isn't made by running on empty—it's made by learning how to fuel yourself properly.

And I don't just mean the basics—sleep, food, movement

(though those do ***actually*** work, shocking, I know). I mean the deeper stuff. The mental, emotional, and strategic ways we generate momentum and keep it going.

Because let me tell you, I used to do it all wrong.

## The Torture of Trying to Be Consistent

For most of my life, I treated productivity like a moral obligation. If I wasn't performing at 100%, I felt like I was failing. I pushed myself hard—too hard. If I woke up feeling low-energy, I would berate myself for being lazy. If my brain wasn't cooperating, I would force myself to sit in front of my laptop for hours, accomplishing nothing except feeling guilty. **It was torment.**

I didn't realize I was setting myself up for failure by trying to operate like a machine—like someone who experiences consistent energy levels every single day. But I don't. My brain *doesn't* work that way. And now that I *know* that, I've stopped trying to force it.

I've have a new system— an AuDHD hack. Instead of trying to stick to a rigid, one-size-fits-all schedule, I now have *three* different schedules: one for low-energy days, one for medium-energy days, and one for high-energy days.

On high-energy days, I work at full speed. I take on deep work, creative projects, and the hardest problem-solving tasks. I schedule brainstorming sessions, client meetings, and presentations on these days because I know I'll be mentally sharp and at my best.

On medium-energy days, I focus on maintenance tasks—emails, admin work, minor coding fixes, and research. I can still get things done, but I don't push myself to the limit.

And on low-energy days, I give myself permission to slow down. I focus on learning, reading, and small, easy wins. If I need rest, I *take it*. I don't fight against my body anymore—**I work *with* it.**

This system has changed everything. Instead of constantly battling myself, I've found a way to *stay consistent while still honoring my body's needs*. And the best part? I'm actually *more* productive than ever. Because I'm not wasting time beating myself up, forcing myself through tasks when I have nothing to give, or burning out by pushing beyond my limits.

For the first time, I've found balance. I've stopped fighting my energy, and I've started flowing with it. And that's what real success looks like—not just achieving more, but doing it in a way that doesn't destroy you in the process.

## The Power of Knowing What You Want

There's something powerful about getting clear on what you want. Not just vague ideas, not just what you *think* you should want, but what you *truly* desire. The life you see for yourself when no one is watching. The life that feels expansive, aligned, and deeply fulfilling.

For me, that vision led me straight to AI at iOCO. One day, I was pitching a partnership deal to iOCO so that we could work on computer vision projects together, completely immersed in the possibilities of what technology could do for South African enterprise businesses. I had no intention of taking a job—I was too caught up in the thrill of re-building. But then came **Nicole Adriaans**, a woman whose presence instantly commanded respect—not in an aggressive way, but in that rare, effortless kind of leadership. She carried a kind of inner peace that was as sharp as it was soft, and you could tell within minutes of speaking to her that she had mastered the art of balance.

She saw something in me that I wasn't seeing in myself. She didn't have to sell me on the opportunity—she made me see clearly that this was where I was meant to be. She convinced me to take the leap, and just like that, I stepped into a dream role as **Principal AI Consultant at iOCO.**

## Go Where You Are Appreciated, Not Just Tolerated

One of the biggest lessons I've learned is that you can't force people to see your value. If you have to constantly prove your worth, you're in the wrong room. I spent too much of my life trying to fit into spaces that didn't recognize my potential, hoping that if I just worked harder, over-delivered, and made myself smaller, then maybe—just maybe—I would be **fully accepted**. But the truth is, you don't thrive where you're merely tolerated. You thrive where you are ***appreciated***.

In spaces where you are valued, your ideas are heard, your presence is respected, and your growth is encouraged. In places where you are merely tolerated, you will always feel like you are fighting for a seat at a table that was **never meant for you**.

It took me years to understand that real success is about **alignment**, not forced effort. When you are in the right place, you won't have to convince anyone that you belong there.

## The Art of Saying No

One of the most powerful things I ever learned was how to **say no**. Saying no is not about rejecting opportunities—it's about **protecting your energy** and focusing on what truly matters. Every time you say yes to something that doesn't align with your goals, you are saying no to something that does.

I used to say yes to everything—every opportunity, request, and project. I was afraid that saying no would make me seem ungrateful, that doors would close, and that people would think I wasn't willing to work hard enough.

But in reality, saying yes to everything was the fastest way to burn out.

The moment I started saying no to things that didn't align with me, I started experiencing real growth. I wasn't just busy—I was *effective*. I wasn't just doing work—I was *making an impact.*

## Fixing the Country, One AI Model at a Time

As a Principal AI Consultant, my daily work involves **solving complex problems** using AI and helping South African businesses remain globally competitive. I work on large, impactful projects for well-known state-owned enterprises, optimizing systems, using data more effectively, and ensuring that AI isn't just a buzzword but a tool for transformation.

**Fixing the country, one AI model at a time.** <3

I love the challenge, the strategy, and the innovation, but what I love even more is the purpose behind it. AI isn't about replacing people—it's about ***enhancing*** what humans can do. It's about creating opportunities, solving inefficiencies, and making businesses more sustainable.

## The Power of Energy and Alignment

When you start working on your energy, everything changes. When you take care of yourself, your mind gets sharper. When you set boundaries, your time becomes more valuable. When you align your energy with your goals, **you move through life with more ease, more clarity, more confidence.**

The world tells us to hustle, to grind, to keep going even when we're breaking. But growth isn't just about doing more—it's about ***becoming*** more. So take care of yourself. Get clear on what you want. Put yourself in the right rooms. Say no to distractions.

Say yes to alignment. Trust that everything is happening in divine timing.

And remember: ***You don't have to chase what's already meant for you.***

# 15

# Rocket

There's a version of me that I used to fight against. The part of me that feels too much, questions everything and dreams beyond what seems rational. For a long time, I thought she was the problem. That she needed to be controlled, quieted, reshaped into something more acceptable. But I've come to understand that she was never the problem. She was my **inner child**, my raw, unfiltered self—the part of me I named **Rocket**.

I call her Rocket because she is pure energy, untamed and boundless.

She always wanted to launch at full speed toward everything she loved, but I kept trying to hold her back, to make her smaller, more manageable. I spent years ignoring her, suffocating her under expectations, logic, and the exhausting need to fit in. But here's the thing about energy—it doesn't disappear. It finds a way to push through. And eventually, she did.

## The Battle Between Who You Are and Who You've Been Taught to Be

We all have two versions of ourselves: the person we are at our core and the version we construct to survive the world. Psychologists call this **the battle between the 'id' and the 'higher self.'** The id is raw instinct, emotion, and desire, while the higher self is wisdom, patience, and balance.

For a long time, I thought the goal was to suppress the id—to silence Rocket and let the higher self take full control. But what I've come to realize is that **they're supposed to work together**. The raw energy of Rocket fuels my creativity, my ambition, my passion. My higher self directs it, refines it, and makes sure I don't self-destruct in the process.

Rocket wasn't the problem. **Ignoring her was.**

## Letting Rocket Fly

I've spent my whole life thinking I needed to escape my thoughts, to quiet the chaos in my mind. But what I actually needed to learn was how to see them for what they were—just thoughts, not absolute truths. Not every doubt needed my attention. Not every fear deserved to be entertained. And not every societal expectation was worth meeting. The real challenge wasn't escaping Rocket; it was learning how to ride with her, to trust her instincts while keeping my hands on the steering wheel.

She's the one who made me dream big enough to think I could build an NGO from scratch. She's the one who made me dive into AI when people didn't even understand what it was. She's the one who saw a world beyond what was in front of me and dared to chase it. Suppressing her made me miserable. Embracing her made me unstoppable.

## Rewriting the Narrative

For years, I thought my brain was the problem. That my **AuDHD**, my need to think deeply, my obsessive focus, my high sensitivity—they were obstacles to overcome. But they weren't. They were the **exact tools I needed to succeed.**

I had spent so much energy trying to be "normal" that I never stopped to question why normal was even the goal. Who benefits when we shrink ourselves down? When we silence the parts of us that see beyond the present? **Not us.**

When I started trusting Rocket, I realized she wasn't reckless—she was brilliant. She saw patterns, opportunities, and solutions before anyone else. She wasn't chaotic—she was just **too big for small spaces.**

## The Power of Owning Who You Are

I used to think I had to prove myself. That I had to justify my existence by achieving, producing, and making myself useful to others. But I don't anymore.

I am me. Unapologetically.

I no longer explain myself to people who aren't willing to understand. **I just am.**

And Rocket? **She's finally free.**

# 16

# Stand Up

## Becoming the Leadership

I've always believed that the fight for true prosperity in South Africa is a fight we all have to take part in—together. We cannot just wait for change. We have to be the architects of it.

For years, I spoke about leadership as if it was something separate from me. *"Leadership needs to prioritize economic inclusion". "Leadership needs to invest in young entrepreneurs".* ***"Leadership needs to build a better South Africa."***

Until one day, it hit me.
I ***am*** leadership.

I had been waiting for someone else to fix things, **to step up**, to create change, when in reality, I was already in the room. I was already sitting at the table. I was already influencing policies, leading projects, making decisions that impacted industries.

There was no more *they*—**only we.**

That moment of realization was both empowering and terrifying. It meant there was no savior coming. No perfect leader was going to step in and take charge. ***We are the leaders we have been waiting for.*** And that meant it was time to act accordingly.

## A Thank You to Those Who Made This Possible

Before I get into the work ahead, I want to pause. We focus so much on what is broken in our country that we often forget to acknowledge the victories.

To those who fought for freedom—**thank you.**

To those who sacrificed, who marched, who dreamed of a South Africa where all of us could walk freely, own property, get an education, build a future—**thank you**.

You didn't just fight for freedom. You fought for the opportunities that I have today. The fact that I can build a career in AI, that I can sit in boardrooms where decisions are made, that I can travel freely, that I can exist in spaces where my ancestors were denied entry—none of that would be possible without your sacrifices.

So, even as I critique, even as I demand better, even as I refuse to accept the current state of affairs—I do so from a place of gratitude.

Because freedom ***is* sweet**.

There are moments when I catch myself walking into a luxury hotel for a business meeting, sitting down in a high-rise office, or presenting to a room full of executives, and I think to myself: *They would have never let my grandmother sit here.*

And that reminder **fuels me**.

Because I refuse to let their sacrifices go in vain.

## The Lost Professor and the Power of Identity

One day, while walking through the front entrance of the Wits University science building, I saw a man looking completely lost and quite frightened. Meanwhile, I had just gotten my hair done, so my silky strands were blowing in the wind. I was *feeling myself*, walking confidently and minding my business.

He spotted me and immediately latched onto my warm smile. "Excuse me," he said hesitantly, his accent thick. I quickly realized he was a visiting Master's student from India desperate for some help. Of course, I helped him find his way, and just as I was about to leave, he asked curiously, "Are you South African Indian?"

Without missing a beat, I replied, "No, I'm Zulu." And then

I left him standing there, utterly confused. Listen, I wasn't lying! I *am* mostly Zulu. On both sides. But also Portuguese, Indian, Scottish, Khoisan, and, of course, English. I have books, pictures, and stories of my great-grandparents to prove it. ***Mixed masala.***

It wasn't that I was ashamed to look Indian; it was something else that bothered me about the interaction.

Why do we stick to "**our own kind**"? Did he approach me because I was friendly or because I "looked" Indian that day? Probably both. But something about how he asked made it clear—it was more about appearance. As if my identity should be placed in a predefined box for him to understand. That moment didn't offend me, but it lingered. It reminded me how deeply conditioned we are to seek familiarity, to categorize each other instead of simply connecting.

We naturally gravitate toward people who look and think like us. It's instinct—the need for familiarity, the need for belonging. However, by doing so, we are going against our higher potential as humans. We are closing ourselves off from learning and collaboration.

As someone with AuDHD, I've always questioned human behavior from a deeply analytical perspective. Our cave-dwelling ancestors saw differences as threats to survival, but we no longer fight over scarce resources in the same way. The instinct remains, but is it serving us? Or is it holding us back?

## What Does It Mean to Be Coloured?

Being coloured in South Africa means being part of one of the most diverse, vibrant, and culturally rich communities in the world.

It is not just an identity—it is a fusion of histories, languages, and traditions that defied every attempt to erase them. It is resilience and adaptability, a culture that was never meant to exist but refuses to disappear.

We are the descendants of Khoi-San, Malays, Indians, Africans, and Europeans. This mix created a culture that is uniquely ours—one that thrives in music, food, language, and community.

It is the rhythm of Cape Jazz.

It is the spice of a perfectly made Durban curry.

It is the laughter that echoes through a family gathering.

It is speaking English, Afrikaans, or any of the country's other languages, but with a distinct flavour that can never be replicated.

It is Sunday kos with koesisters. It is sharing a gatsby with friends. It is singing and dancing at family gatherings. It is playing R&B while cleaning the house. It is a culture born from hardship but bursting with joy.

Wherever you go, family and community mean everything, and no one leaves your house without eating first.

If ancestry was a recipe, mine would have every ingredient on the shelf. I come from Portuguese sailors who traveled the world, English and Scottish settlers who made a new life here, and Indian ancestors who brought their rich traditions, spices, and entrepreneurial spirit to South African shores. The strength of the Zulu and Swazi runs through me. The Khoi-San—the first storytellers of this land—are woven into my DNA.

I am the product of explorers, warriors, survivors, and dreamers.

We are a people who adapt, who make something out of nothing, who bring flavour to everything we touch. Our history isn't just about struggle—it's about innovation, creativity, and joy.

We are a community that takes life seriously but laughs even harder, that turns pain into poetry and everyday moments into celebrations.

I am a walking story of everything that has come before me. I carry a thousand stories in my blood.

And every single one leads to this:

**I am South African.**

## The Work Ahead: We Are Not Angry Enough

One of my favorite South African comedians, Eugene Khoza, said something to me at an event while I was editing this chapter.

*"We are not angry enough."*

And he's right.

**We *should* be angry.** We should be angry that after 30 years of democracy, people still don't have access to clean water. That unemployment is still gut-wrenchingly high. That corruption is still robbing futures. That GBV is a daily reality.

But here's the thing—anger alone doesn't build a future. ***Action does.***

And that's why, despite the frustration, struggle, and exhaustion, I keep standing up.

And **you can too.**

# 17

# Eternal Sunshine

**Healing is such a strange thing.** For the longest time, I thought it was a journey with a clear destination. I imagined it like a staircase—something you climb, step by step, until you reach the top, look around, and declare, *I'm healed.*

But healing doesn't work like that.

There was no singular moment when I suddenly felt lighter, when the old wounds stopped aching, when my nervous system stopped bracing for impact. It happened quietly. Subtly.

One day, I noticed that my body wasn't always tense. One day, I caught myself smiling for no reason. One day, I woke up and my first thought wasn't, *What needs fixing?*

It turns out healing is less like climbing a staircase and more like the sun slowly rising. You don't notice it is happening in real time, but then suddenly, everything is bright.

I was born free. But now? **I actually feel free.**

## Eternal Sunshine

The first version of this book was raw—almost too raw. It was the kind of writing that spills out when you finally let yourself acknowledge the weight of everything you've carried. In many ways, it was a trauma dump. My family and friends were shaken when they read it, blindsided by the full force of what I had endured. But I don't regret writing that version. It needed to exist. It was the ultimate journaling experience—an unfiltered release of everything I had never fully said out loud.

But then came the editing. And with it, a shift. I had to ask myself: *Is this the story I want to put into the world?*

Healing is not just about surviving what happened to you—it's about reclaiming the narrative. It's about choosing what you take forward.

This book will have done its job if, in reading it, just one person finds a piece of themselves they thought was lost. If one person sees their own struggles with softer eyes, knowing that survival is not just about endurance but about transformation. If just one person reads this and finds the strength to move forward, to smile through their own healing, to see themselves with more love and less shame. If just one person feels lighter, freer, more hopeful—then I have succeeded.

The real healing happened in the rewriting. I saw my story differently—not as a series of wounds, but as proof of resilience. Not as a weight to carry, but as wisdom earned. And that's when I understood: It's not what happens to us that defines us, but what we choose to do with it.

There is power in how you tell your story. It shapes the way you see yourself. It shapes the way you move forward. And when I knew, deep in my bones, that I had truly healed, I realized something profound:

The only things that remained were the good—the lessons, the laughter, the growth, the light.

## The Weight Is Gone

I didn't just heal from AuDHD burnout. I healed from all of it. The weight of expectation. The constant need to prove myself. The exhaustion of carrying my coloured identity in a country that struggles to define it. The pressure of being a woman in a world that demands softness and strength in impossible proportions.

For years, I felt like I was constantly navigating a battlefield. Trying to be taken seriously in tech. Trying to hold my own in rooms where my expertise was questioned before I even spoke. Trying to balance ambition with the expectation of what a woman *should* want.

But I have nothing left to prove.

Not to society. Not to men.
Not to colleagues.
Not even to myself.
**I can just *be*.**

## Endless Possibilities

There is something exhilarating about realizing that your life is yours again. That nothing is tying you down—not expectations, not self-doubt, not even your own limiting beliefs.

So what now?

**Anything.**

**Everything.**

For the first time in my life, I have no rigid plan, no desperate need to control the outcome. I have no idea where life will take me, and I've never been more at peace with that. Maybe I'll write more. Maybe I'll dive deeper into AI. Maybe I'll explore something completely unexpected. Maybe, just maybe, I'll even lean into my birthday prophecy and find my way into politics. The point is, I can do whatever I want. ***I am free*.**

## The Sweetness of Freedom

**Freedom is sweet.**

The kind of sweetness that lingers. The kind that is fully savored after years of hunger. I am free from the noise in my head that told me I wasn't enough. I am free from the need to chase validation. I am free from the fear of failing. I am free from the exhaustion of constantly explaining myself. I am free from the lie that being single means being incomplete. I am free from the belief that my empathy is a weakness.

And that freedom? It tastes better than anything money, success, or romance could ever offer.

I was born free. **But now, I live free.**

So what's left for me to do?

**Be.**

**Then think.**

**Then do.**

*Passionately so.*

# Journal Prompts for Reflection

## Introduction to Journaling: A Journey Through Reflection

This is not just a book—it's an experience. As you read through each chapter, you'll notice that this isn't just about my story. It's about the universal truths that we all encounter, the lessons we learn, and the growth we embrace. That's why I've included journaling prompts—to turn this book into something more than just words on a page.

Journaling is powerful. It's a tool for self-reflection, a mirror to your thoughts, and a way to process life in a deeper, more intentional way. It helps clarify emotions, unlock creativity, and even reduce anxiety. It's not about writing something perfect—it's about showing up for yourself on the page. So, as you move through this book, don't just read. Experience. Light a candle. Play the song that goes with each chapter. Let yourself feel. And then, when you're ready, pick up your journal and start writing. There's no right or wrong way to do this. Just be honest with yourself. Let the words flow. This is your space. Your journey. Your truth.

## Journal Prompts for Each Chapter

### *Chapter 1: Isn't she lovely*

1. What is a lesson you learned the hard way that has shaped who you are today?
2. If you could give advice to your younger self, what would you say?
3. Think about a challenge you once thought was impossible. How did you overcome it?
4. What beliefs about yourself have changed over time?
5. What is something you know for sure *now* that you didn't know five years ago?

### *Chapter 2: What a difference a day makes*

1. When was the last time you said yes to something you didn't actually want to do? How did it make you feel?
2. What is something (or someone) you need to say no to in your life right now?
3. How do you handle guilt when setting boundaries?
4. Think of a time when saying no protected your energy. What happened?
5. What would change in your life if you confidently embraced the power of no?

### *Chapter 3: Gramercy Park*

1. Have you ever felt like you had to shrink yourself to fit in? Describe that experience.
2. What is a part of you that others have called "too much,"

but you secretly love?
3. How has self-doubt held you back from something you really wanted?
4. What's one "crazy" dream you've always had but never pursued?
5. What would happen if you fully embraced who you are, without fear of judgment?

## *Chapter 4: Human*

1. Think of a time you had to start over. How did it feel, and what did you learn?
2. What does resilience mean to you? How have you shown it in your own life?
3. Write about a setback that turned out to be a blessing in disguise.
4. How do you handle failure? Do you see it as an end or a beginning?
5. What is something you want to come back stronger from right now?

## *Chapter 5: Truth or Dare*

1. What was a defining moment in your life when you had to take a risk?
2. Have you ever chosen stability over passion? How did that decision impact you?
3. What fears hold you back from pursuing your wildest dreams?
4. What does success look like *to you*—not society, not your family, just you?

5. If you had no fear, what's the first dare you would take in your life right now?

## *Chapter 6: Feel the need*

1. Who is a woman in your life that has inspired you? Write about her impact.
2. How has your upbringing shaped the way you view success and failure?
3. What is something you feel called to do but haven't yet pursued?
4. If you could create change in your community, what would you focus on?
5. What's one lesson from your ancestors that still guides you today?

## *Chapter 7: Touch the Sky*

1. Have you ever felt like you had to prove yourself more because of your gender?
2. What would the world look like if more women were in leadership positions?
3. Have you ever been underestimated? How did you respond?
4. What does empowerment mean to you, and how do you empower yourself?
5. If you could mentor a younger version of yourself, what lessons would you share?

## *Chapter 8: Her light*

1. What is a basic need in your life that you've been neglecting?
2. What is your relationship with money, and how has it shaped your decisions?
3. How do you handle uncertainty? Do you resist it or embrace it?
4. What is something you need to walk away from to create space for something new?
5. How do you define success outside of career and financial achievements?

## *Chapter 9: Samba Pa Ti*

1. Have you ever achieved something you thought would make you happy, but it didn't?
2. What does fulfillment look like to you beyond external success?
3. How do you know when you're on the right path in life?
4. If you could design a life that truly excites you, what would it look like?
5. How do you balance ambition with peace?

## *Chapter 10: Vienna*

1. What is something you've been holding onto that you need to let go of?
2. Have you ever had to start over? How did you rebuild?
3. How do you handle change? Do you resist it or welcome it?
4. What is one risk you want to take but haven't yet?

5. What advice would you give to someone going through a major life transition?

### *Chapter 11: Don't You Worry 'Bout a Thing*

1. What's one thing you've overcome that once felt impossible?
2. How do you manage stress and anxiety in your daily life?
3. Write about a time you found joy even in the midst of chaos.
4. What does resilience mean to you? How do you cultivate it?
5. How can you remind yourself to trust the process, even when things feel uncertain?

### *Chapter 12: Energy*

1. What drains your energy the most, and how can you protect yourself from it?
2. What activities make you feel the most alive?
3. How do you recharge when you're feeling depleted?
4. What boundaries do you need to set to protect your energy?
5. How can you be more intentional about where you invest your time and effort?

### *Chapter 13: Table for Three*

1. How has your view on love and relationships changed over time?
2. What qualities do you value most in a partner?
3. Have you ever lost yourself in a relationship? How did you find your way back?

4. How do you show love to yourself?
5. What is one thing you've learned about love that you wish everyone knew?

## Chapter 14: Becoming

1. What version of yourself are you currently growing into?
2. How have your past experiences shaped who you are today?
3. What is something you are unlearning about yourself?
4. How do you practice self-acceptance?
5. What does personal growth mean to you?

## Chapter 15: Rocket

1. Have you ever tried to suppress a part of yourself? Why?
2. What is something about yourself that you're learning to embrace?
3. How do you balance instinct and logic when making decisions?
4. What is a childhood dream you want to reconnect with?
5. If you could let yourself be fully free, what would that look like?

## Chapter 16: Stand Up

1. What does leadership mean to you?
2. How can you step up more in your own life?
3. What is one change you wish to see in your country or community?
4. Have you ever doubted your ability to lead? Why?
5. What legacy do you want to leave behind?

*Chapter 17: Eternal Sunshine*

1. What does healing look like for you?
2. How do you measure your own growth?
3. What is something you've let go of that no longer serves you?
4. What is one thing you want to forgive yourself for?
5. How do you practice self-love in your daily life?

## This book was never just about my journey—it was about yours, too.

Growth isn't a destination, and healing isn't linear. The biggest shifts happen in the quiet moments, in the way you show up for yourself daily. So, as you close this book, take a breath. Reflect. Trust that you are exactly where you need to be.

You don't have to have it all figured out.

Just keep showing up.

For yourself.

For your dreams.

For the life that's waiting for you.

**This is just the beginning.**

www.ingramcontent.com/pod-product-compliance
Lightning Source LLC
Chambersburg PA
CBHW071344230926
51846CB00002B/436
*9781991269577*